POP SO
FOR KIDS

MW00559777

ISBN 978-1-5400-9496-4

Visit Hal Leonard Online at
www.halleonard.com

Contact us:
Hal Leonard
7777 West Bluemound Road
Milwaukee, WI 53213
Email: info@halleonard.com

In Europe, contact:
Hal Leonard Europe Limited
42 Wigmore Street
Marylebone, London, W1U 2RN
Email: info@halleonardeurope.com

In Australia, contact:
Hal Leonard Australia Pty. Ltd.
4 Lentara Court
Cheltenham, Victoria, 3192 Australia
Email: info@halleonard.com.au

Adore You

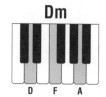 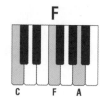 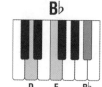 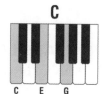

Words and Music by Harry Styles,
Thomas Hull, Tyler Johnson
and Amy Allen

Moderate Pop Rock

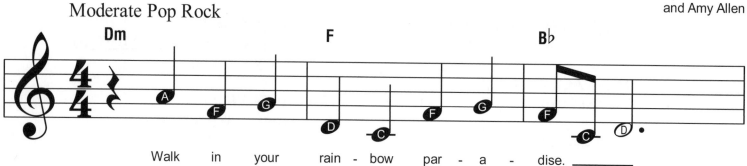

Walk in your rain-bow par-a-dise. _____

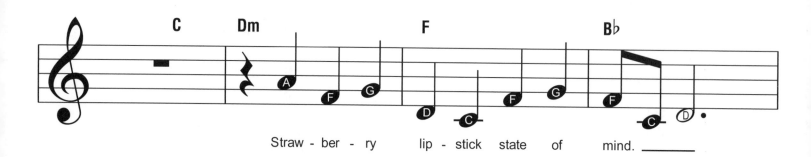

Straw-ber-ry lip-stick state of mind. _____

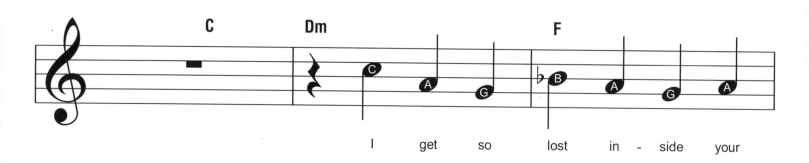

I get so lost in-side your

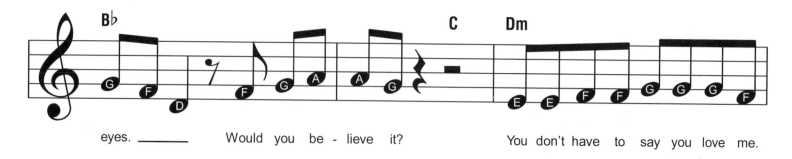

eyes. _____ Would you be-lieve it? You don't have to say you love me.

5

Bad Day

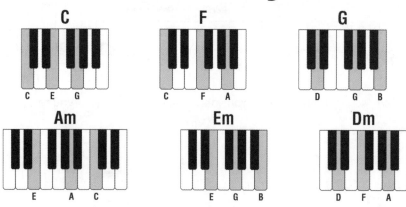

Words and Music by
Daniel Powter

Moderate Shuffle

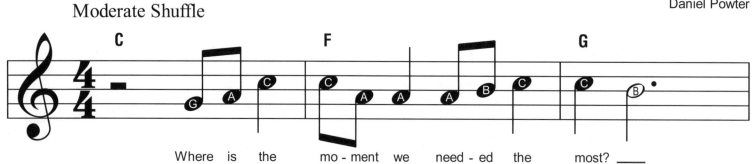

Where is the mo - ment we need - ed the most? ____

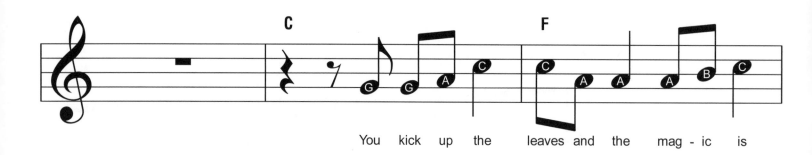

You kick up the leaves and the mag - ic is

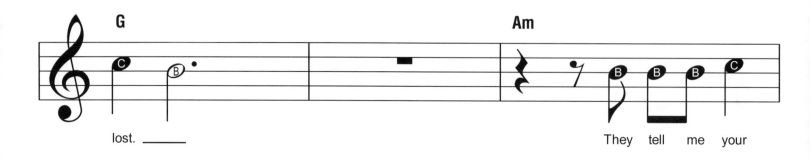

lost. ____ They tell me your

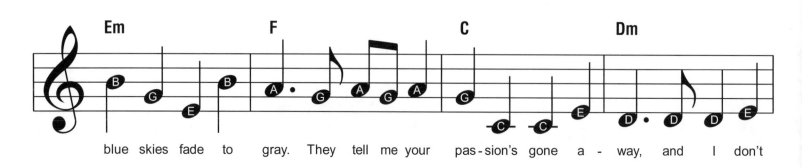

blue skies fade to gray. They tell me your pas - sion's gone a - way, and I don't

7

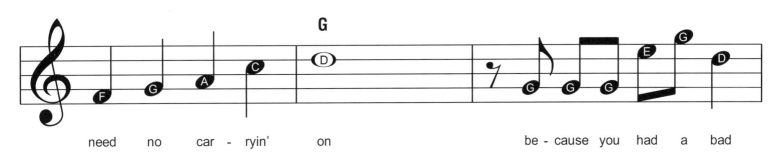

need no car - ryin' on   be - cause you had a bad

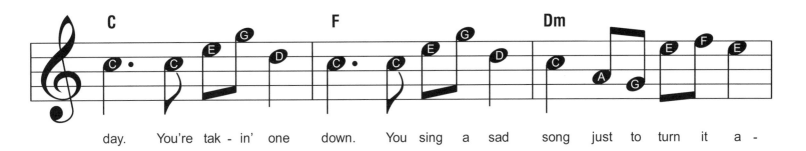

day.   You're tak - in' one   down.   You sing a sad   song just to turn it a -

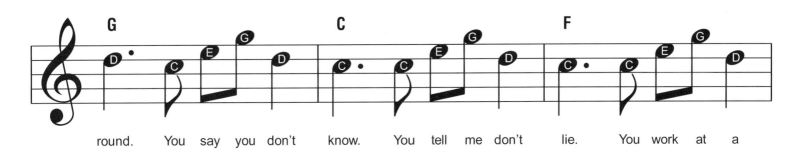

round.   You say you don't   know.   You tell me don't   lie.   You work at a

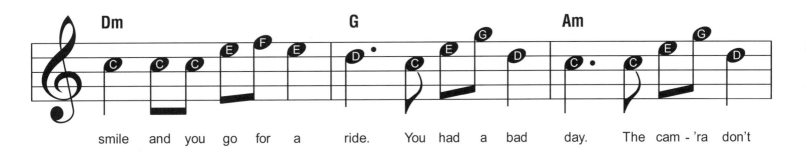

smile and you go for a   ride.   You had a bad   day.   The cam - 'ra don't

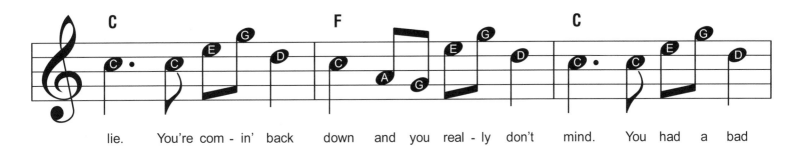

lie.   You're com - in' back   down and you real - ly don't   mind.   You had a bad

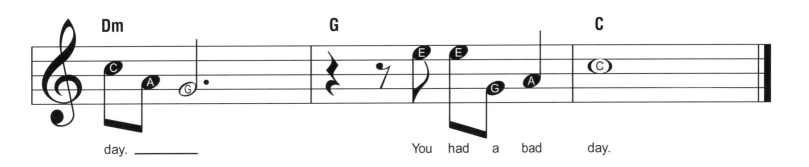

day. _____   You had a bad   day.

Bang!

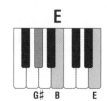
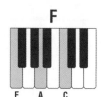
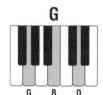
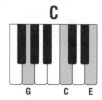

Words and Music by Adam Metzger,
Jack Metzger and Ryan Metzger

Half-time Shuffle

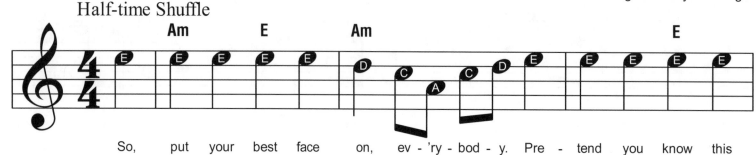

So, put your best face on, ev-'ry-bod-y. Pre-tend you know this

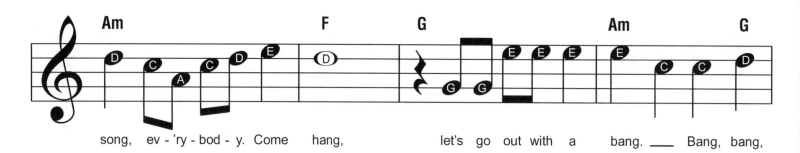

song, ev-'ry-bod-y. Come hang, let's go out with a bang. ___ Bang, bang,

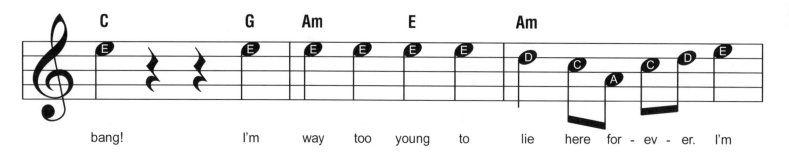

bang! I'm way too young to lie here for-ev-er. I'm

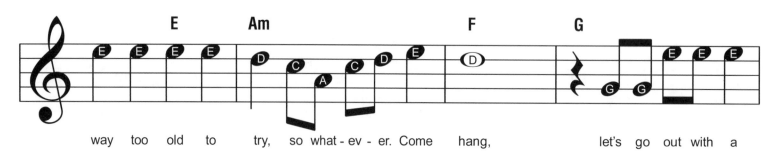

way too old to try, so what-ev-er. Come hang, let's go out with a

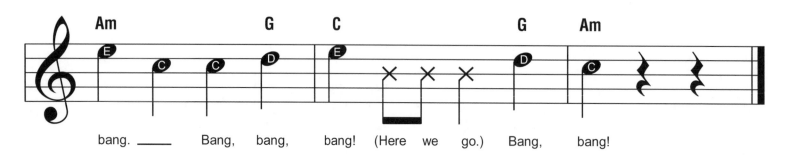

bang. ___ Bang, bang, bang! (Here we go.) Bang, bang!

Drivers License

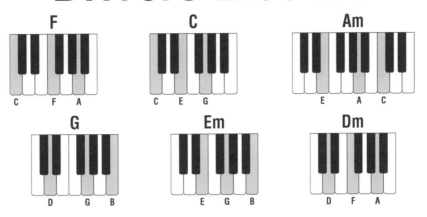

Words and Music by Olivia Rodrigo
and Daniel Nigro

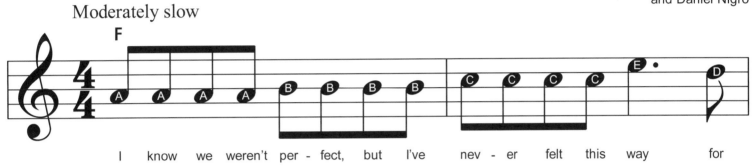

I know we weren't per-fect, but I've nev-er felt this way for

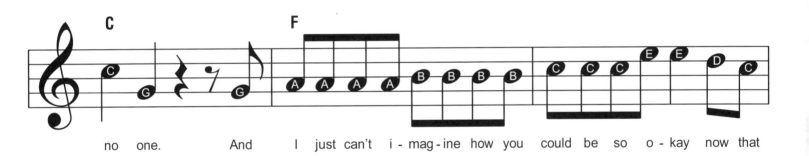

no one. And I just can't i-mag-ine how you could be so o-kay now that

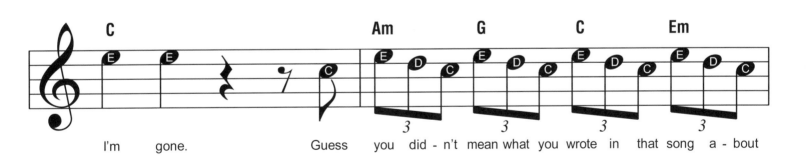

I'm gone. Guess you did-n't mean what you wrote in that song a-bout

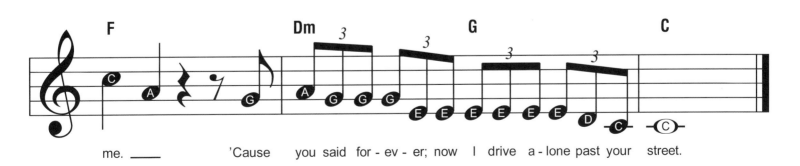

me. _____ 'Cause you said for-ev-er; now I drive a-lone past your street.

Best Day of My Life

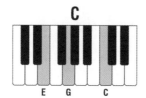
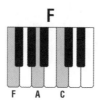
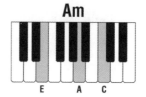

Words and Music by Zachary Barnett,
James Adam Shelley, Matthew Sanchez,
David Rublin, Shep Goodman
and Aaron Accetta

Happily

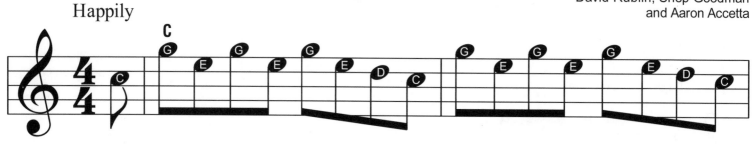

I had a dream so big and loud, I jumped so high I touched the clouds. _

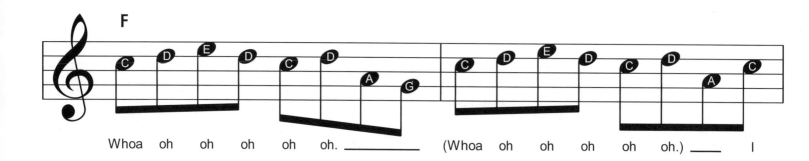

Whoa oh oh oh oh oh. _____ (Whoa oh oh oh oh oh.) _____ I

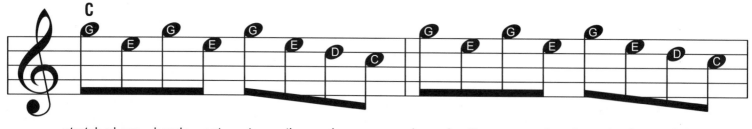

stretched my hands out to the sky, we danced with mon - sters through the night. _

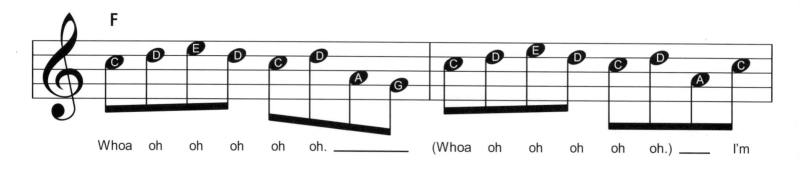

Whoa oh oh oh oh oh. _____ (Whoa oh oh oh oh oh.) _____ I'm

Better Days

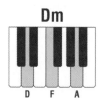 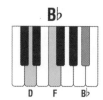 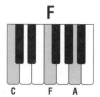

Words and Music by Ryan Tedder,
Brent Kutzle and John Nathaniel

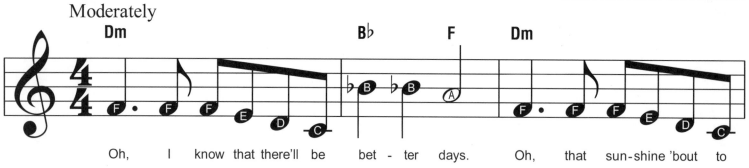

Oh, I know that there'll be bet-ter days. Oh, that sun-shine 'bout to

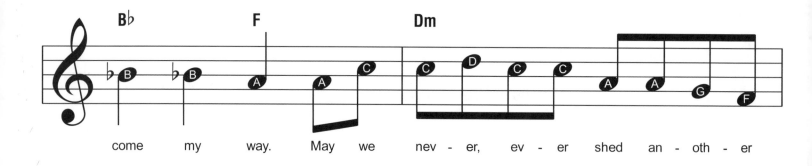

come my way. May we nev-er, ev-er shed an-oth-er

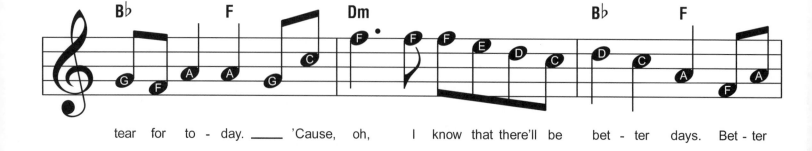

tear for to-day. ____ 'Cause, oh, I know that there'll be bet-ter days. Bet-ter

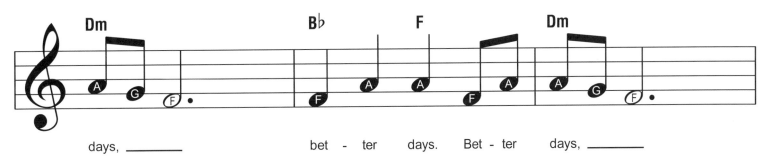

days, _____ bet - ter days. Bet - ter days, _____

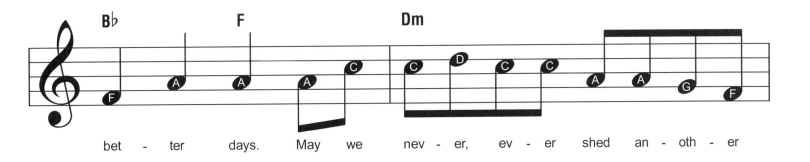

bet - ter days. May we nev - er, ev - er shed an - oth - er

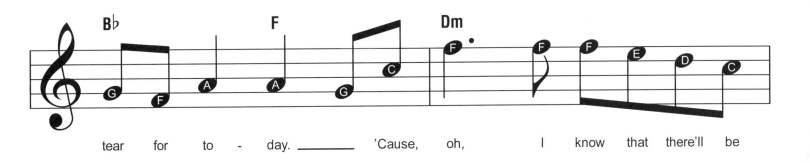

tear for to - day. _____ 'Cause, oh, I know that there'll be

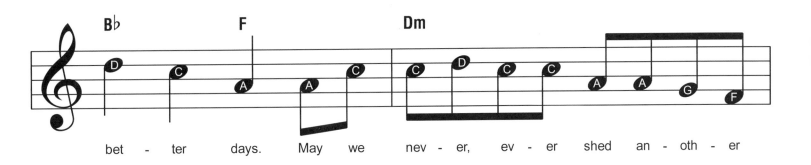

bet - ter days. May we nev - er, ev - er shed an - oth - er

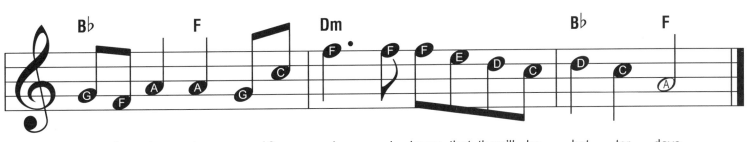

tear for to - day. ___ 'Cause, oh, I know that there'll be bet - ter days.

Brave

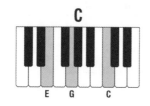 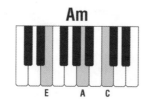 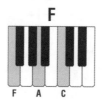

Words and Music by Sara Bareilles
and Jack Antonoff

Moderately

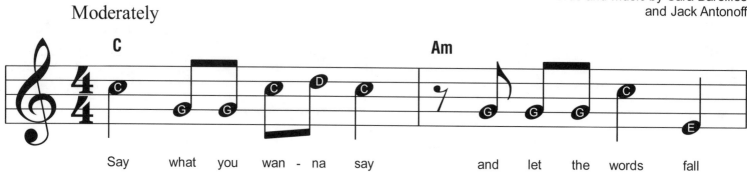

Say what you wan - na say and let the words fall

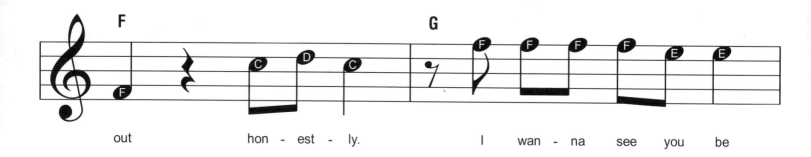

out hon - est - ly. I wan - na see you be

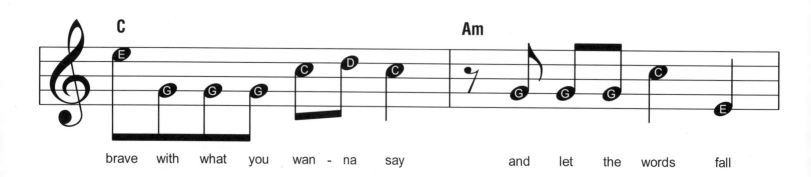

brave with what you wan - na say and let the words fall

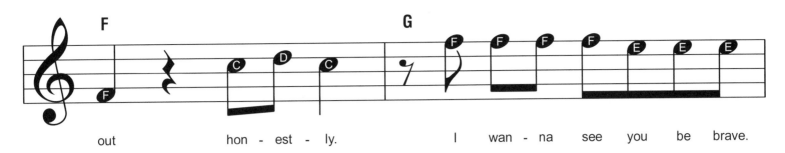

out   hon - est - ly.   I   wan - na   see   you   be   brave.

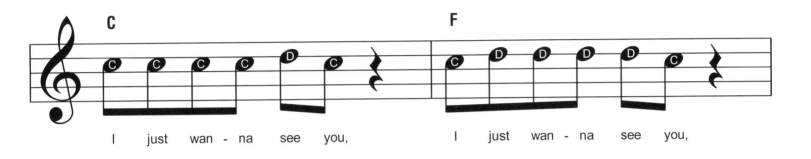

I   just   wan - na   see   you,   I   just   wan - na   see   you,

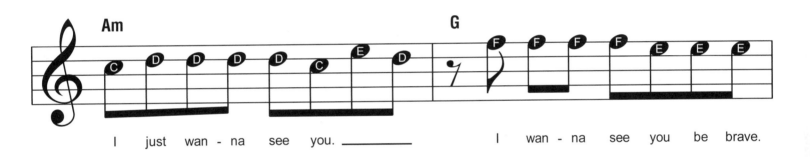

I   just   wan - na   see   you. _____   I   wan - na   see   you   be   brave.

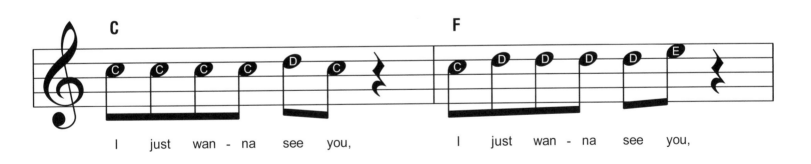

I   just   wan - na   see   you,   I   just   wan - na   see   you,

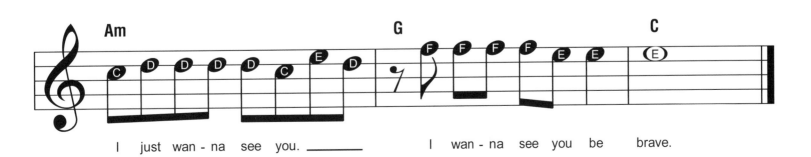

I   just   wan - na   see   you. _____   I   wan - na   see   you   be   brave.

Call Me Maybe

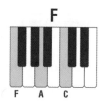
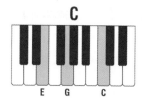
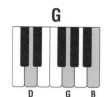
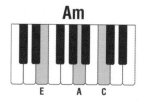

Words and Music by Carly Rae Jepsen,
Joshua Ramsay and Tavish Crowe

Moderately fast

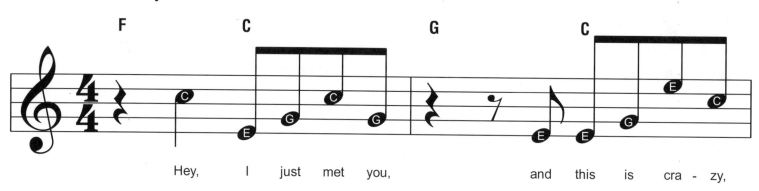

Hey, I just met you, and this is cra - zy,

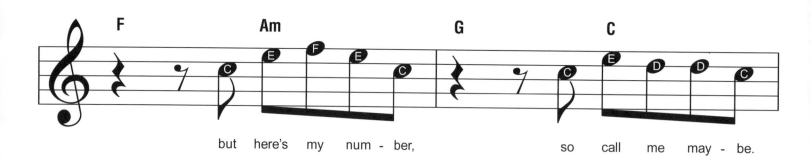

but here's my num - ber, so call me may - be.

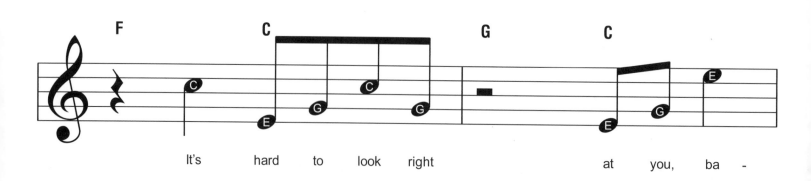

It's hard to look right at you, ba -

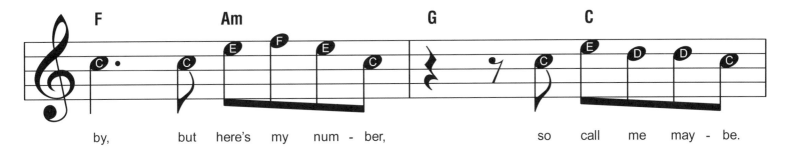

by, but here's my num - ber, so call me may - be.

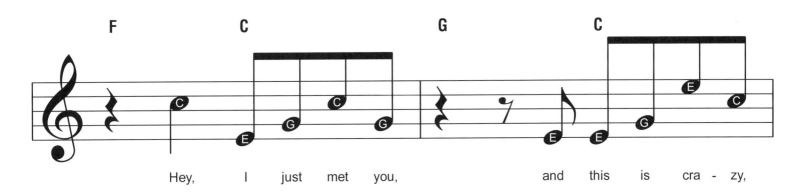

Hey, I just met you, and this is cra - zy,

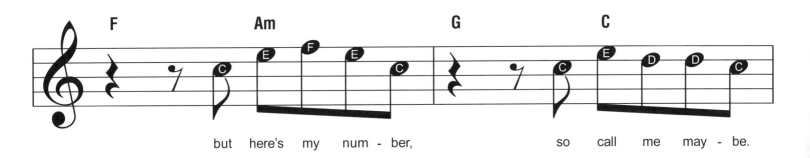

but here's my num - ber, so call me may - be.

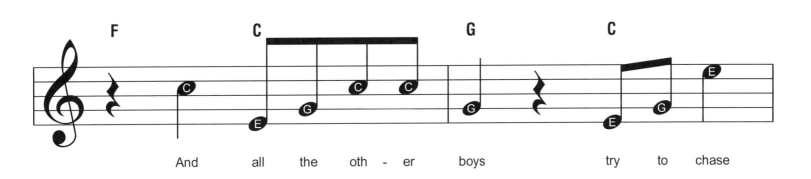

And all the oth - er boys try to chase

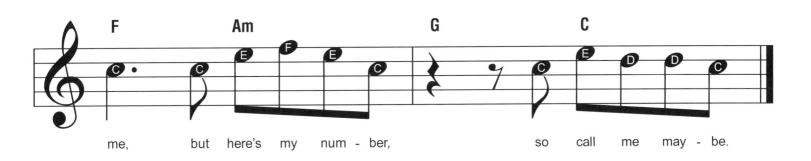

me, but here's my num - ber, so call me may - be.

Can't Stop the Feeling!
from TROLLS

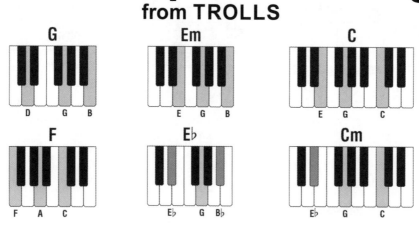

Words and Music by Justin Timberlake,
Max Martin and Shellback

Cool Kids

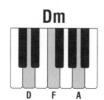 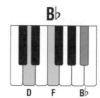 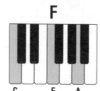 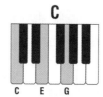

Words and Music by Graham Sierota,
Jamie Sierota, Noah Sierota,
Sydney Sierota, Jeffrey David Sierota
and Jesiah Dzwonek

Moderately fast

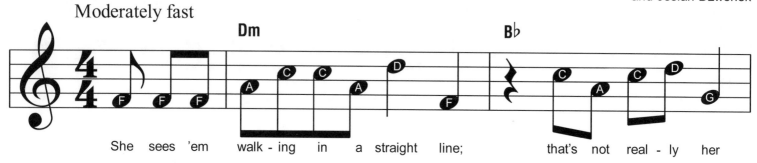

She sees 'em walk-ing in a straight line; that's not real-ly her

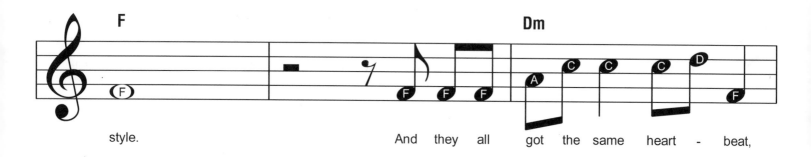

style. And they all got the same heart-beat,

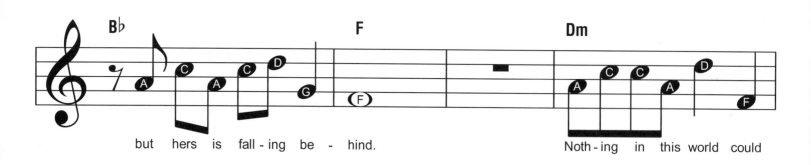

but hers is fall-ing be-hind. Noth-ing in this world could

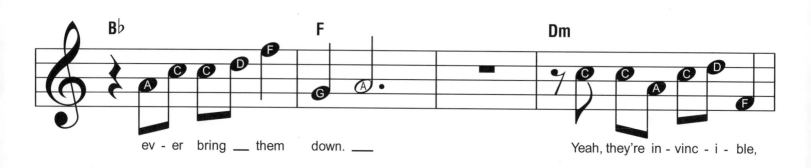

ev-er bring them down. Yeah, they're in-vinc-i-ble,

21

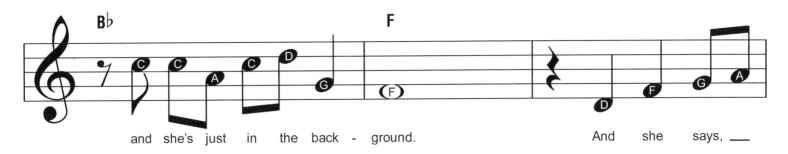

and she's just in the back - ground. And she says, ___

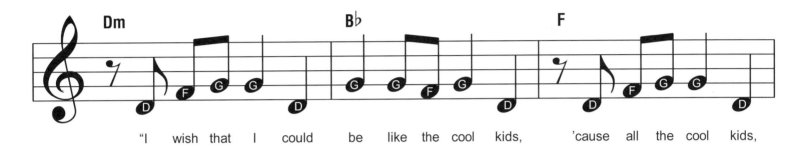

"I wish that I could be like the cool kids, 'cause all the cool kids,

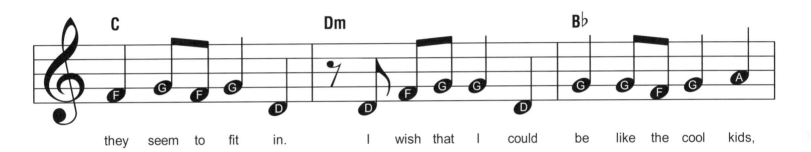

they seem to fit in. I wish that I could be like the cool kids,

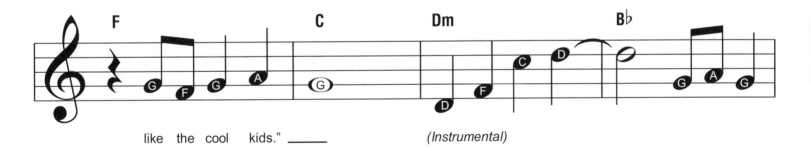

like the cool kids." ___ *(Instrumental)*

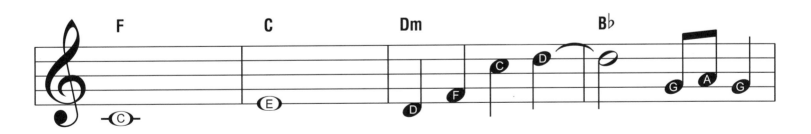

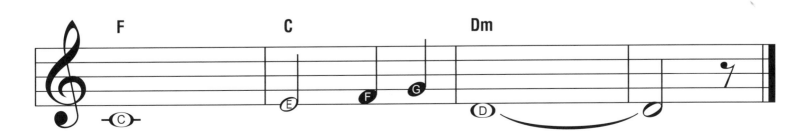

Dance Monkey

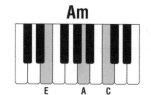
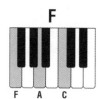
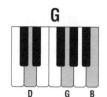

Words and Music by
Toni Watson

Dynamite

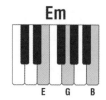 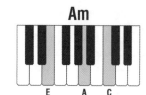 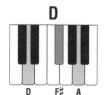 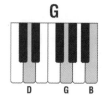

Words and Music by Jessica Agombar
and David Stewart

Moderately fast

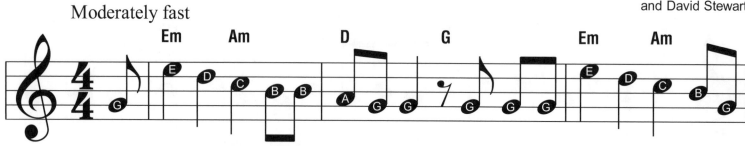

'Cause I, I, I'm in the stars to-night, so watch me bring the fire, set the

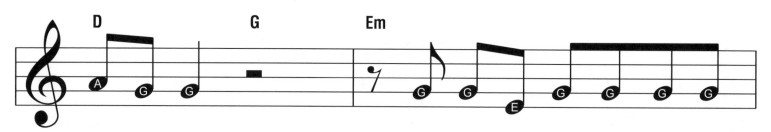

night a-light. Show's on, I get up in the morn, cup of

milk, let's rock and roll. King Kong, kick the drum, roll-ing

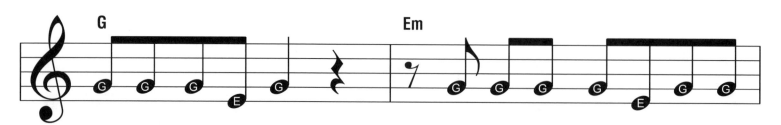

on like a Roll-ing Stone. Sing song when I'm walk-ing home, jump

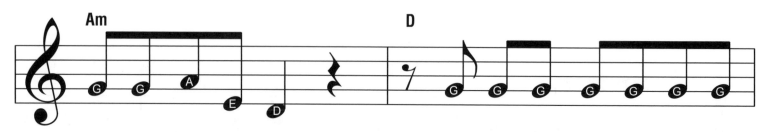

up to the top, Le-Bron. Ding-dong, call me on my phone, iced

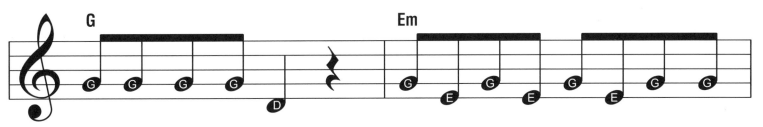

tea and a game of Ping - Pong. This is get - ting heav - y; can you hear the

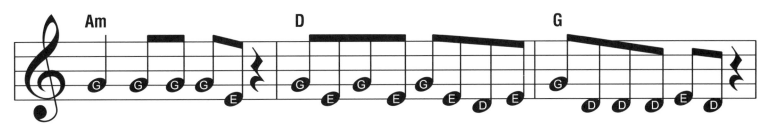

bass boom? I'm read - y. Life is sweet as hon - ey, yeah, this beat, cha-ching like mon - ey.

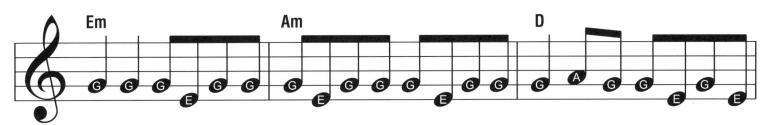

Dis - co o - ver-load, I'm in - to that, I'm good to go. I'm dia - mond; you know I glow up.

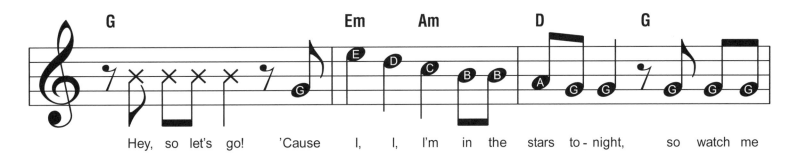

Hey, so let's go! 'Cause I, I, I'm in the stars to - night, so watch me

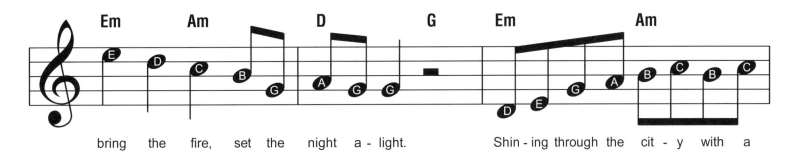

bring the fire, set the night a - light. Shin - ing through the cit - y with a

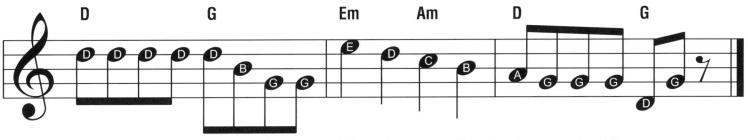

lit - tle funk and soul. __ I'm - a light it up like dy - na - mite. Whoa. _____

Everything Is Awesome
(Awesome Remixx!!!)
from THE LEGO MOVIE

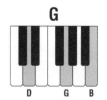 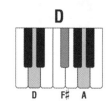 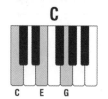 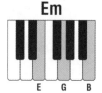 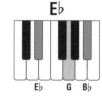

Words by Shawn Patterson
Music by Andrew Samberg,
Jorma Taccone, Akiva Schaffer,
Joshua Bartholomew, Lisa Harriton
and Shawn Patterson

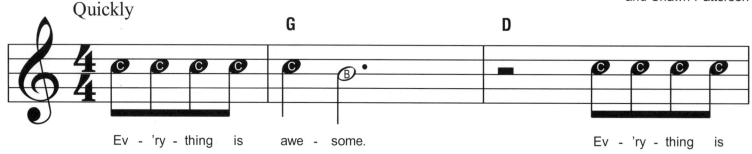

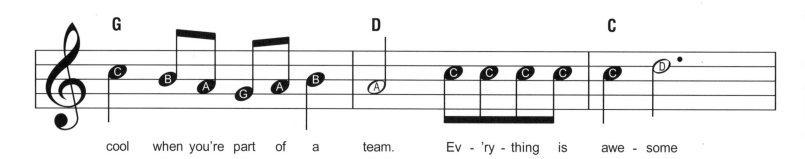

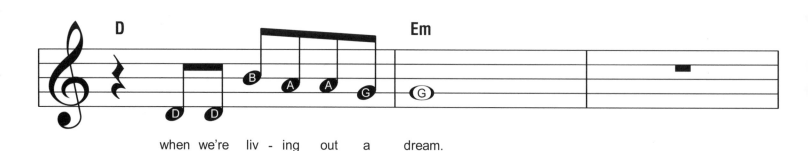

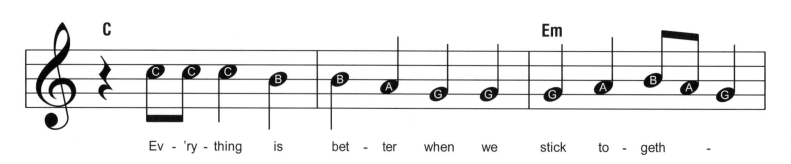

Feel It Still

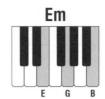 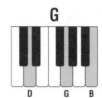 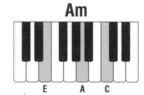

Words and Music by John Gourley,
Zach Carothers, Jason Sechrist,
Eric Howk, Kyle O'Quin,
Brian Holland, Freddie Gorman,
Georgia Dobbins, Robert Bateman,
William Garrett, John Hill and Asa Taccone

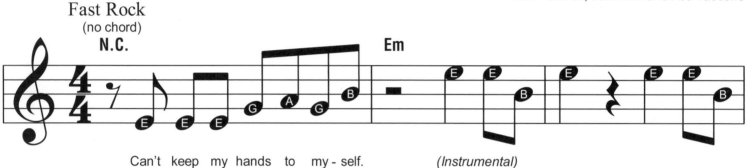

Can't keep my hands to my-self.   (Instrumental)

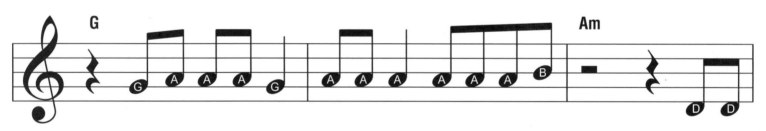

Think I'll dust 'em off, put 'em back up on the shelf,   case my

lit-tle ba-by girl is in need.   Am I com-ing out-a left field?

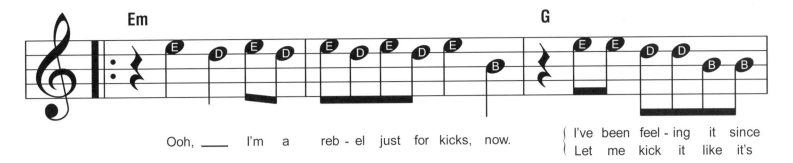

Ooh, _____ I'm a reb - el just for kicks, now.

I've been feel - ing it since
Let me kick it like it's

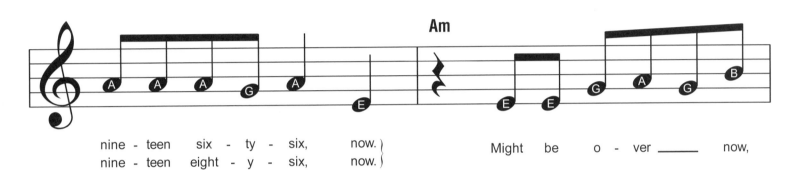

nine - teen six - ty - six, now.
nine - teen eight - y - six, now.

Might be o - ver _____ now,

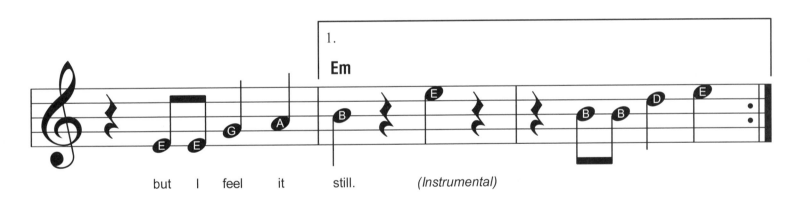

1.

but I feel it still.   (Instrumental)

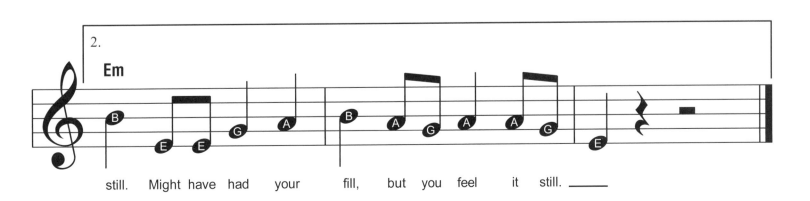

2.

still. Might have had your fill, but you feel it still. _____

Fight Song

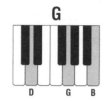 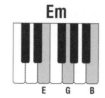 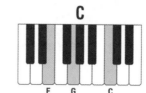 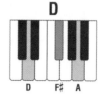

Words and Music by Rachel Platten
and Dave Bassett

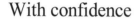

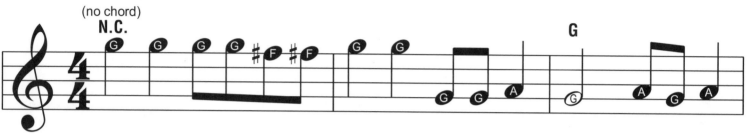

(Instrumental)

Like a small boat on the o -

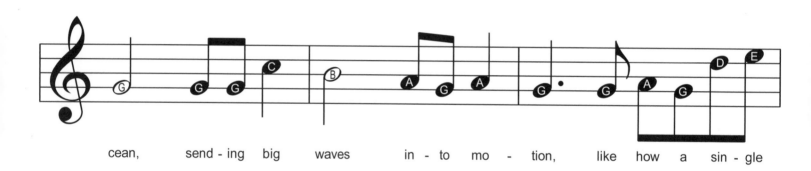

cean, send-ing big waves in - to mo - tion, like how a sin - gle

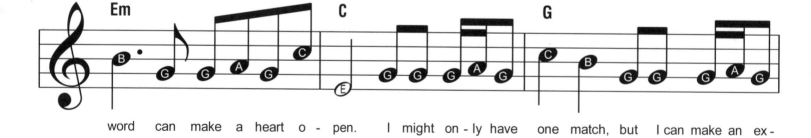

word can make a heart o - pen. I might on - ly have one match, but I can make an ex -

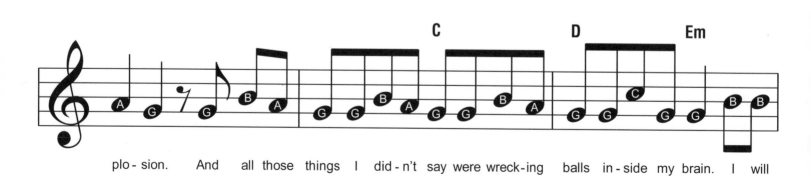

plo - sion. And all those things I did - n't say were wreck-ing balls in - side my brain. I will

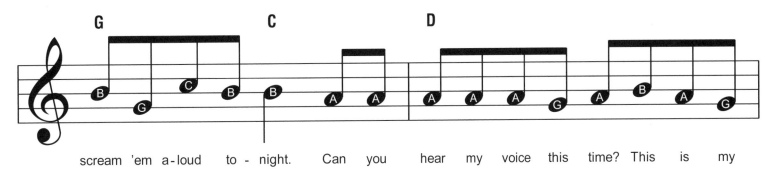

scream 'em a-loud to - night. Can you hear my voice this time? This is my

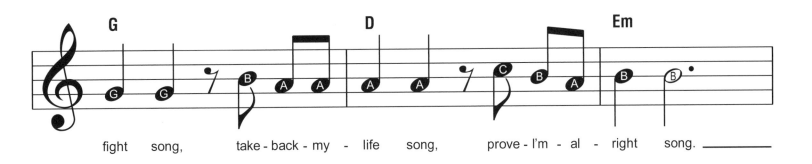

fight song, take-back-my-life song, prove-I'm-al-right song. _____

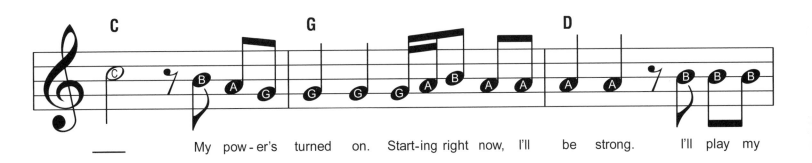

_____ My pow-er's turned on. Start-ing right now, I'll be strong. I'll play my

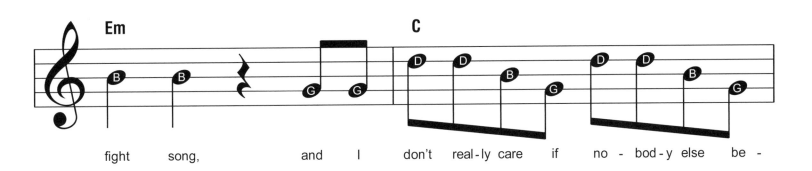

fight song, and I don't real-ly care if no-bod-y else be -

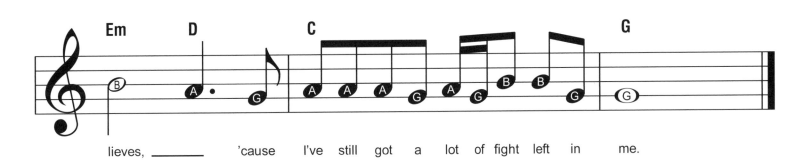

lieves, _____ 'cause I've still got a lot of fight left in me.

Firework

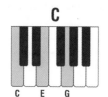 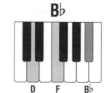 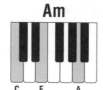 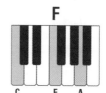 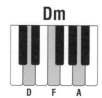

Words and Music by Katy Perry,
Mikkel Eriksen, Tor Erik Hermansen,
Esther Dean and Sandy Wilhelm

Dance Pop

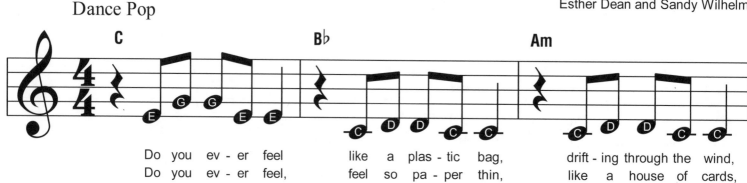

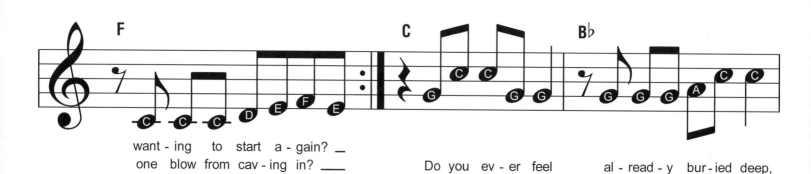

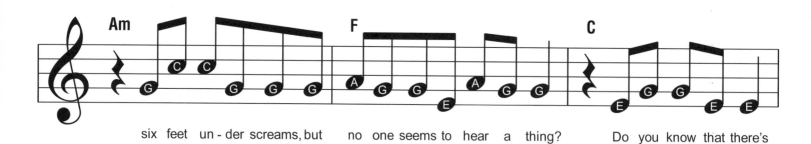

Happier

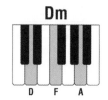
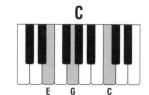
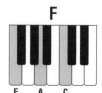
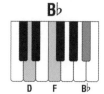

Words and Music by Marshmello,
Steve Mac and Dan Smith

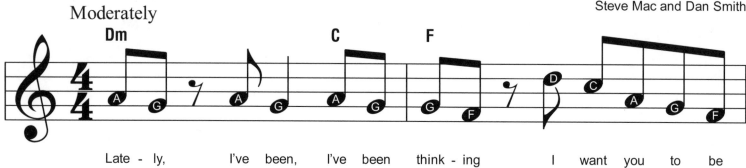

Late - ly, I've been, I've been think - ing I want you to be

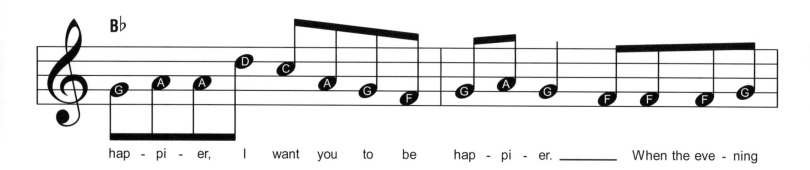

hap - pi - er, I want you to be hap - pi - er. _____ When the eve - ning

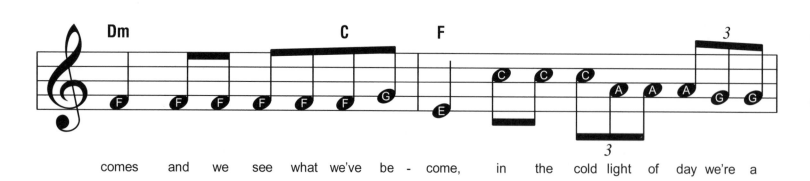

comes and we see what we've be - come, in the cold light of day we're a

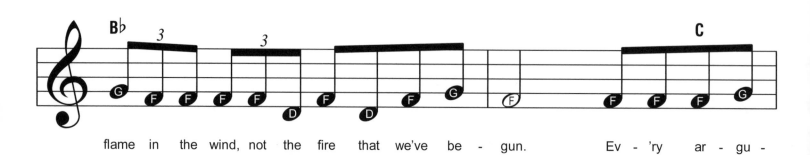

flame in the wind, not the fire that we've be - gun. Ev - 'ry ar - gu -

Happy
from DESPICABLE ME 2

Words and Music by
Pharrell Williams

37

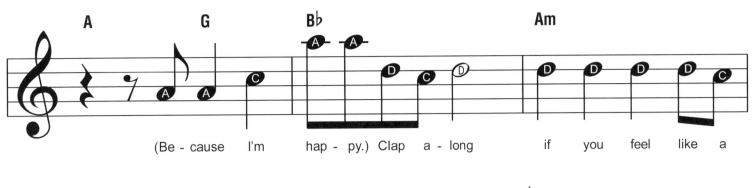

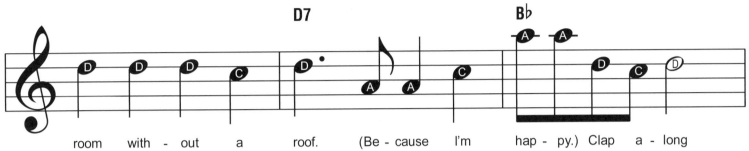

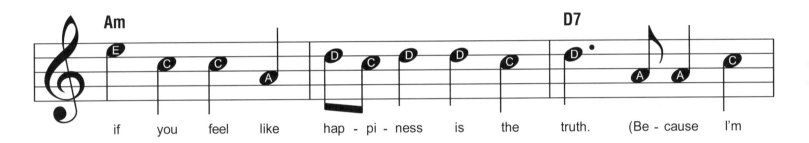

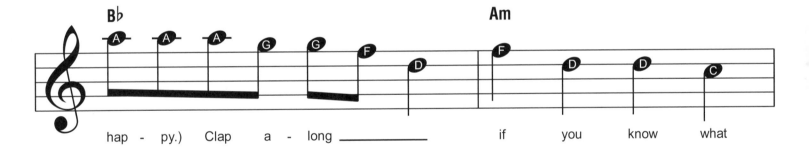

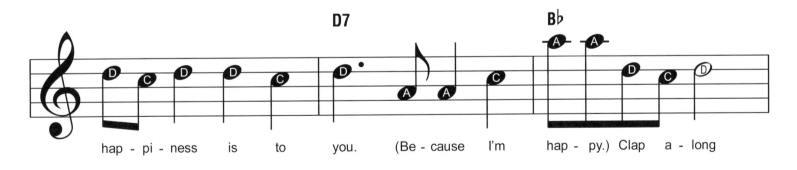

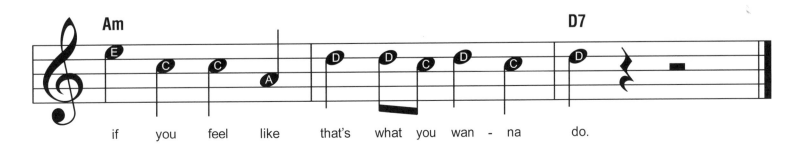

Havana

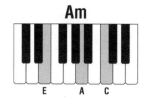
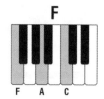
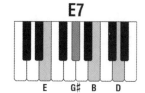

Words and Music by Camila Cabello,
Louis Bell, Pharrell Williams,
Adam Feeney, Ali Tamposi,
Jeffery Lamar Williams, Brian Lee,
Andrew Wotman, Brittany Hazzard
and Kaan Gunesberk

With a Latin groove

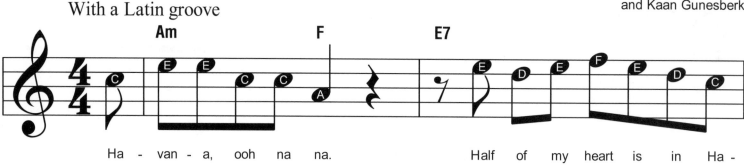

Ha - van - a, ooh na na. Half of my heart is in Ha -

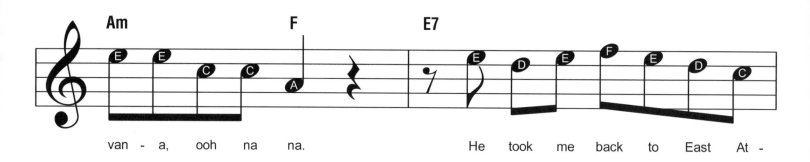

van - a, ooh na na. He took me back to East At -

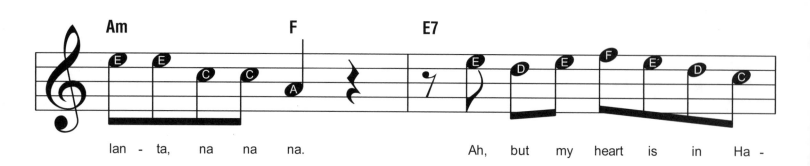

lan - ta, na na na. Ah, but my heart is in Ha -

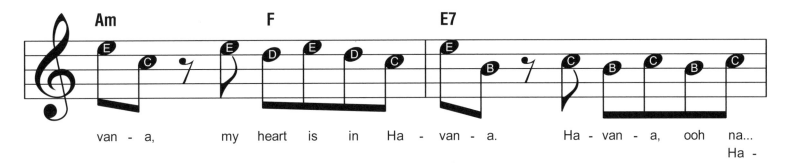

van - a, my heart is in Ha - van - a. Ha - van - a, ooh na... Ha -

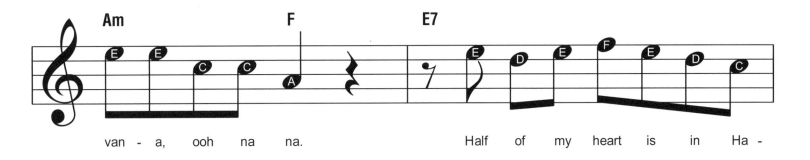

van - a, ooh na na. Half of my heart is in Ha -

van - a, ooh na na. He took me back to East At -

lan - ta, na na na. Ah, but my heart is in Ha -

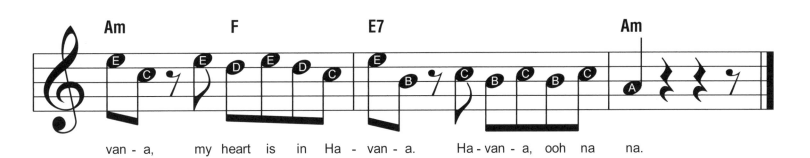

van - a, my heart is in Ha - van - a. Ha - van - a, ooh na na.

High Hopes

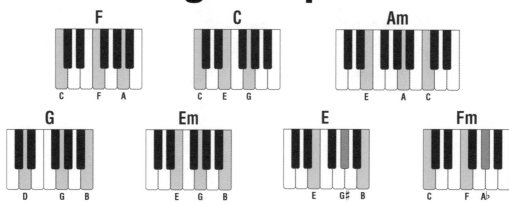

Words and Music by Brendon Urie,
Samuel Hollander, William Lobban Bean,
Jonas Jeberg, Jacob Sinclair,
Jenny Owen Youngs, Ilsey Juber,
Lauren Pritchard and Tayla Parx

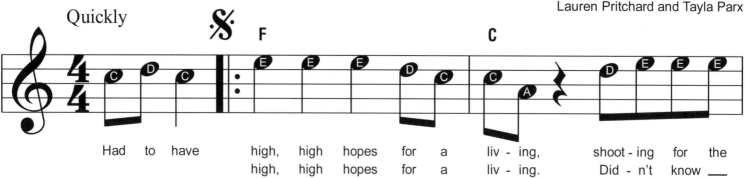

Had to have high, high hopes for a liv-ing, shoot-ing for the
high, high hopes for a liv-ing. Did-n't know ___

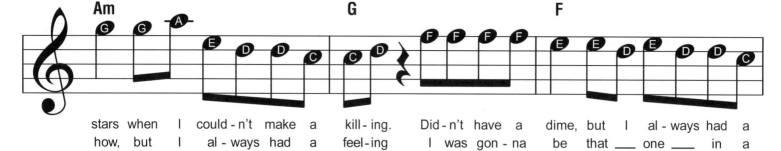

stars when I could-n't make a kill-ing. Did-n't have a dime, but I al-ways had a
how, but I al-ways had a feel-ing I was gon-na be that ___ one ___ in a

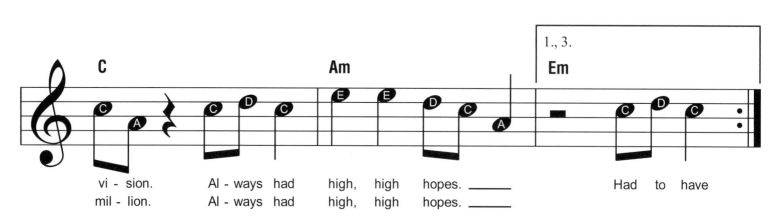

vi-sion. Al-ways had high, high hopes. _____
mil-lion. Al-ways had high, high hopes. _____ Had to have

Home

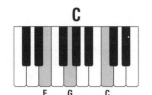 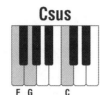 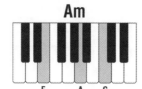 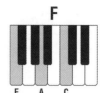 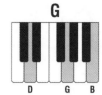

Words and Music by Greg Holden
and Drew Pearson

Brightly

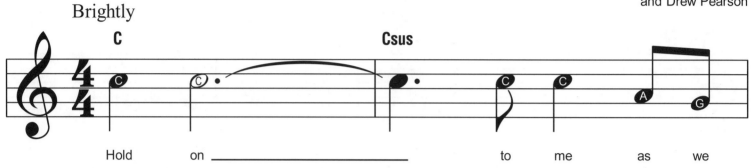

Hold on _____ to me as we

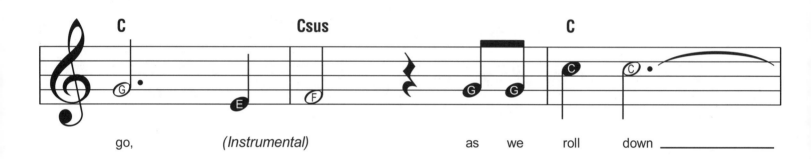

go, (Instrumental) as we roll down _____

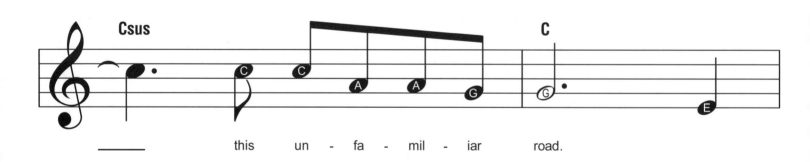

_____ this un - fa - mil - iar road.

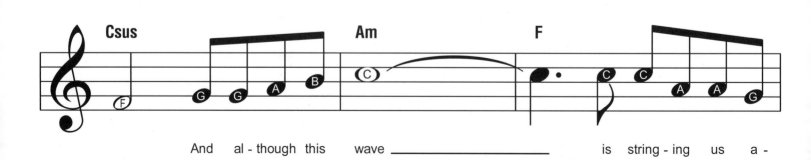

And al - though this wave _____ is string - ing us a -

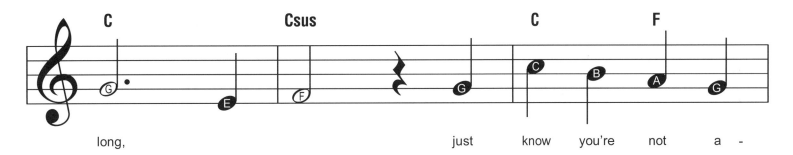

long,   just   know   you're   not   a -

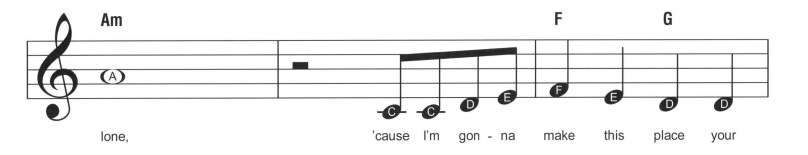

lone,   'cause   I'm   gon - na   make   this   place   your

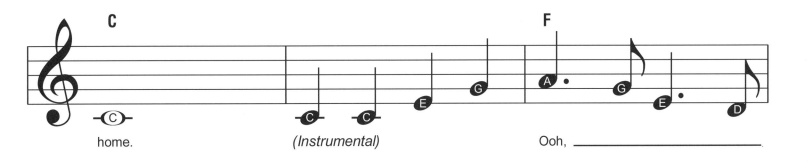

home.   (Instrumental)   Ooh, _____.

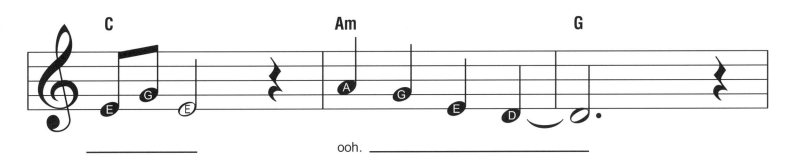

_____   ooh. _____

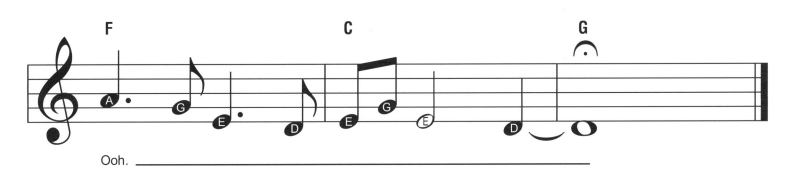

Ooh. _____

House of Gold

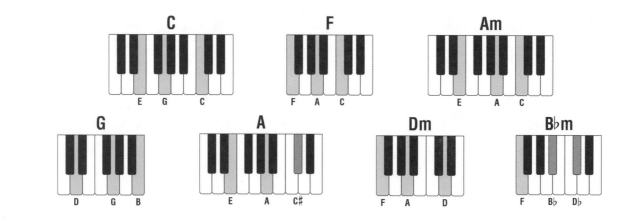

Words and Music by
Tyler Joseph

Moderately bright

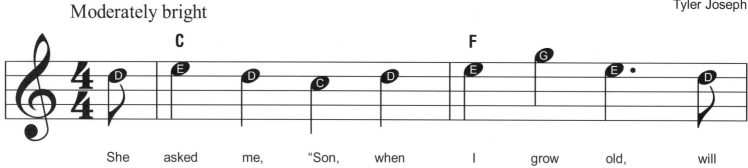

She asked me, "Son, when I grow old, will

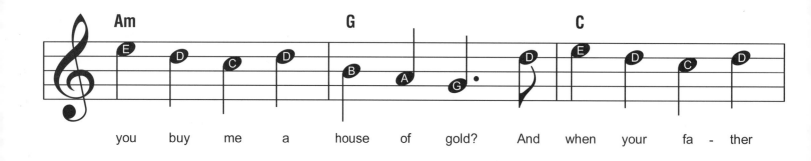

you buy me a house of gold? And when your fa - ther

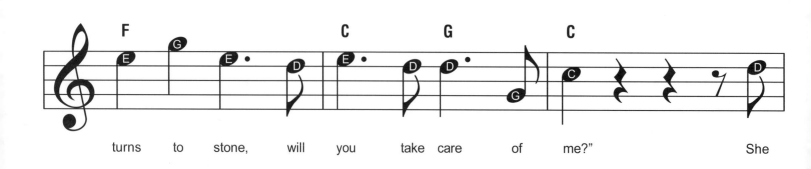

turns to stone, will you take care of me?" She

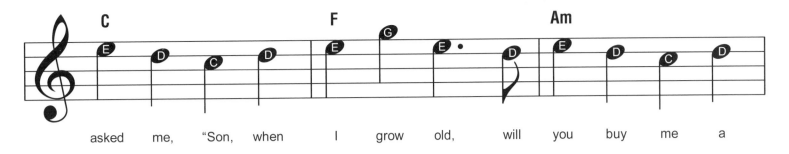

asked me, "Son, when I grow old, will you buy me a

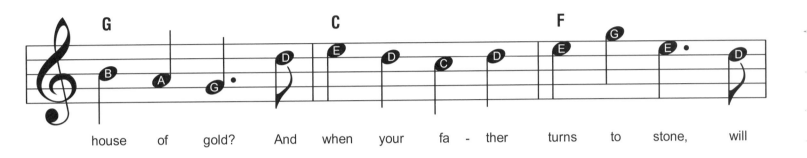

house of gold? And when your fa - ther turns to stone, will

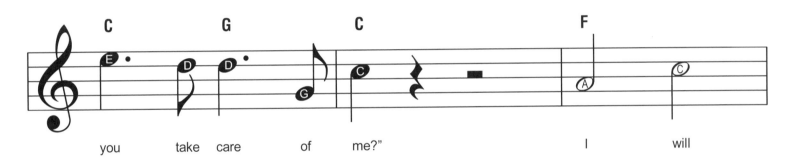

you take care of me?" I will

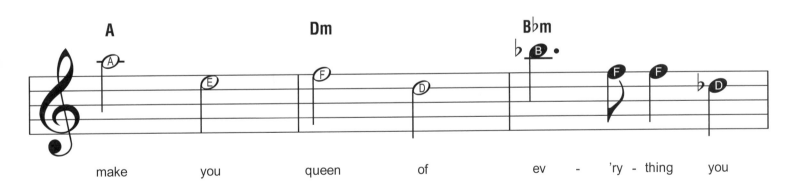

make you queen of ev - 'ry - thing you

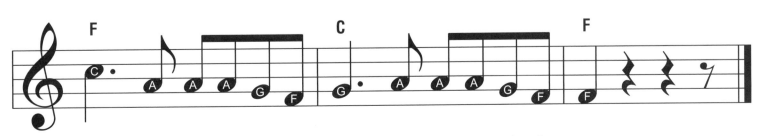

see. I'll put you on the map, I'll cure you of dis - ease.

How Far I'll Go

from MOANA

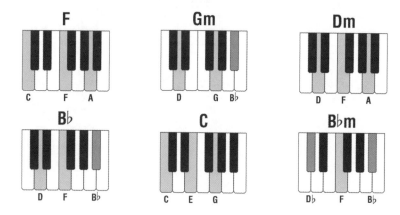

Music and Lyrics by
Lin-Manuel Miranda

Moderate half-time feel

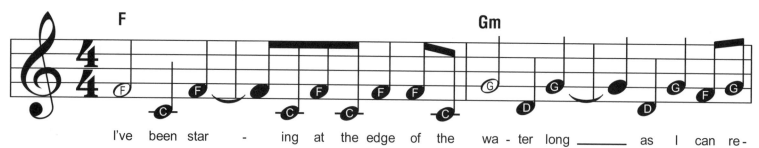

I've been star - ing at the edge of the wa - ter long _____ as I can re-

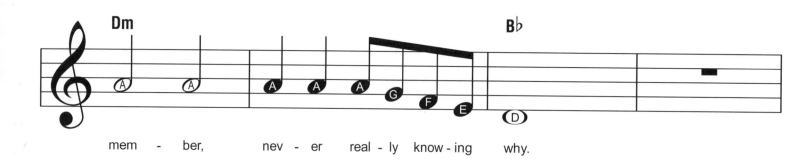

mem - ber, nev - er real - ly know - ing why.

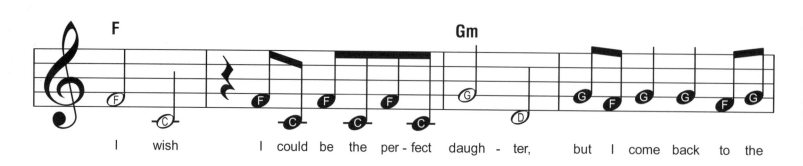

I wish I could be the per - fect daugh - ter, but I come back to the

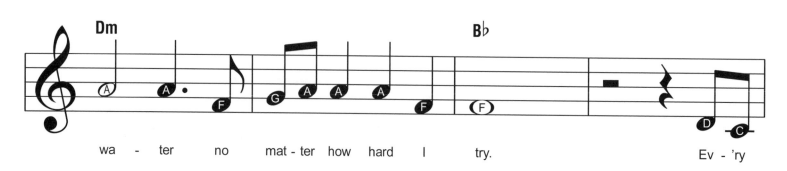

wa - ter no mat - ter how hard I try. Ev - 'ry

I Built a Friend

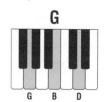 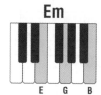 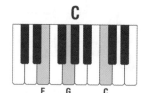 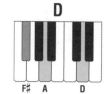

Words and Music by Alec Benjamin
and Brandon Rogers

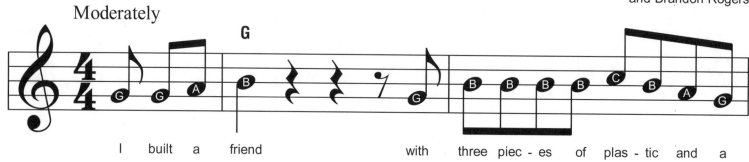

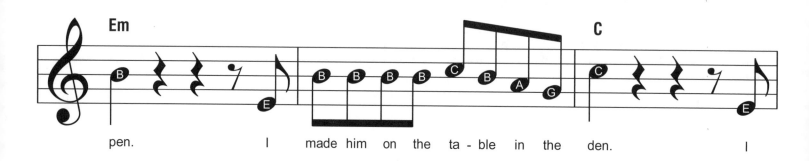

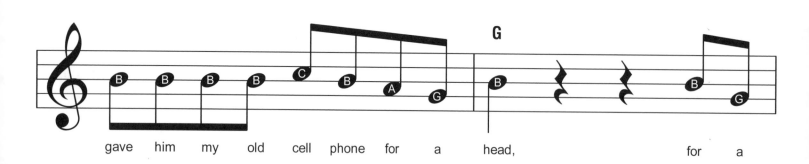

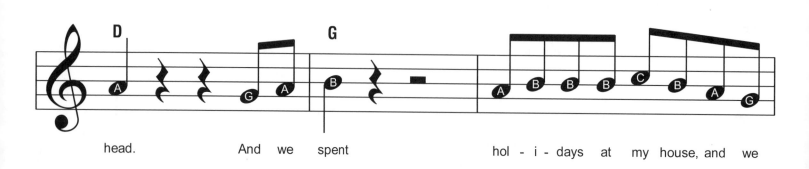

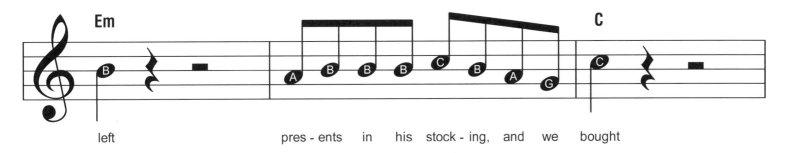

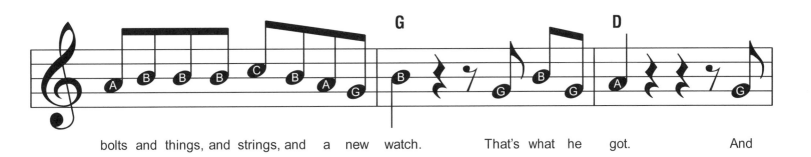

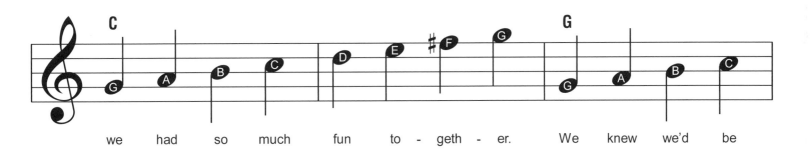

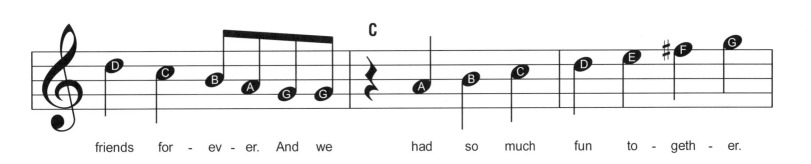

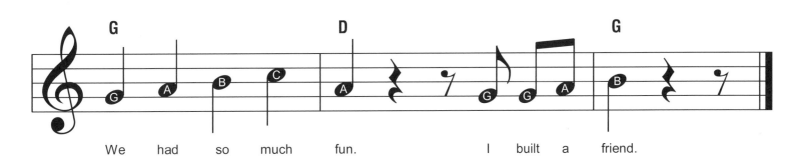

I Don't Know My Name

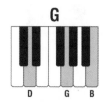
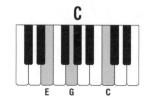
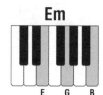
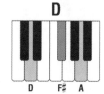

Words and Music by
Grace VanderWaal

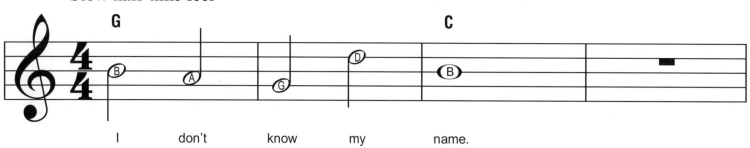

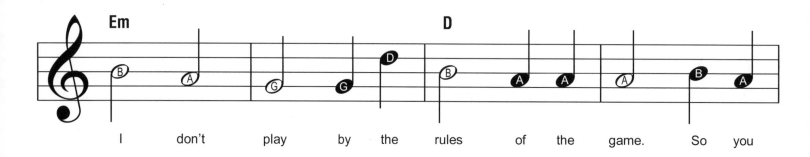

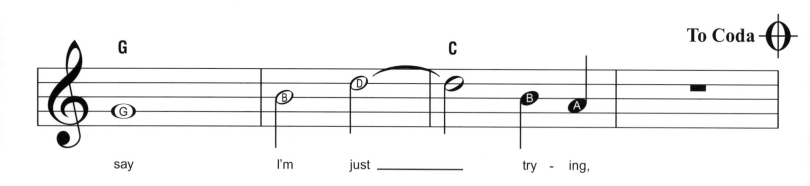

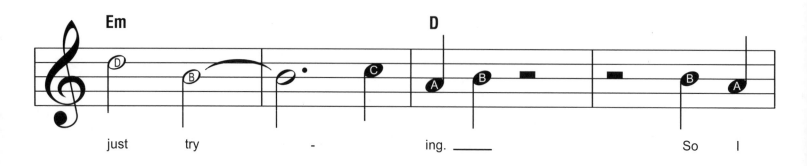

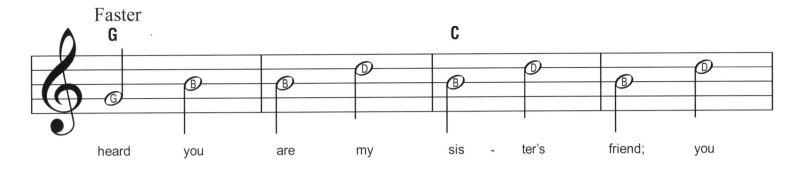

Faster

heard you are my sis - ter's friend; you

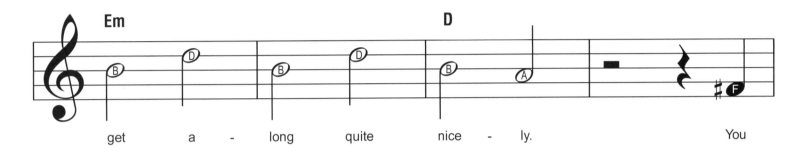

get a - long quite nice - ly. You

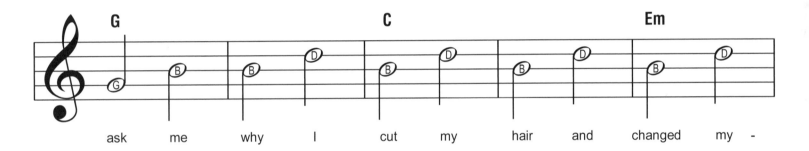

ask me why I cut my hair and changed my -

D.C. al Coda
(Return to beginning,
play to ⊕ and skip to Coda)

CODA

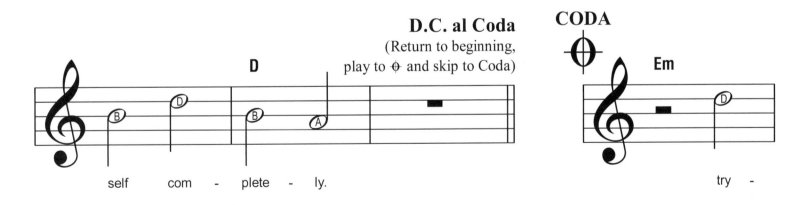

self com - plete - ly.

try -

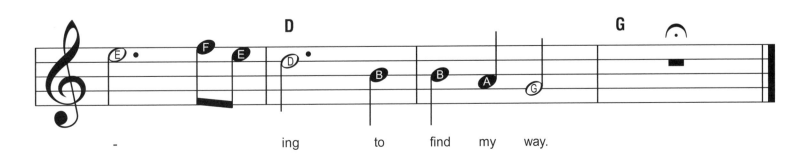

- ing to find my way.

Into the Unknown
from FROZEN 2

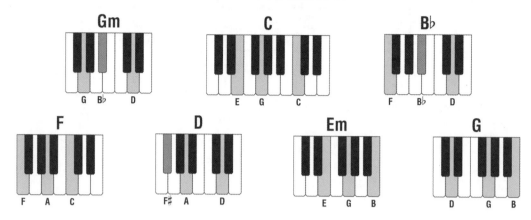

Music and Lyrics by Kristen Anderson-Lopez
and Robert Lopez

With determination

ELSA: You're not a voice; you're just a ring - ing in my

ear. And if I heard you, *(which I don't)* I'm spo - ken for, I fear.

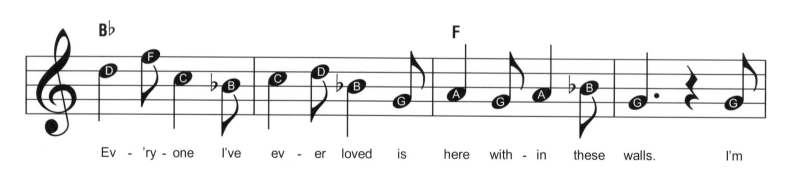

Ev - 'ry - one I've ev - er loved is here with - in these walls. I'm

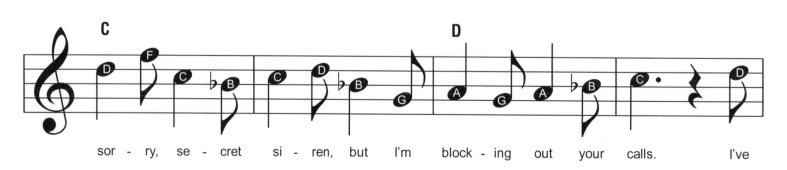

sor - ry, se - cret si - ren, but I'm block - ing out your calls. I've

53

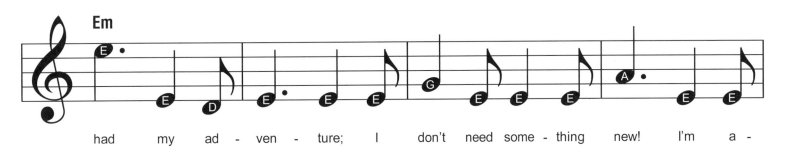

had my ad - ven - ture; I don't need some - thing new! I'm a -

fraid of what I'm risk - ing if I fol - low you in - to the un -

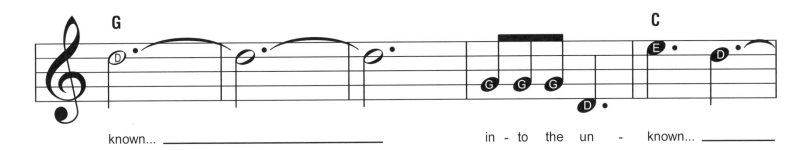

known... _____ in - to the un - known... _____

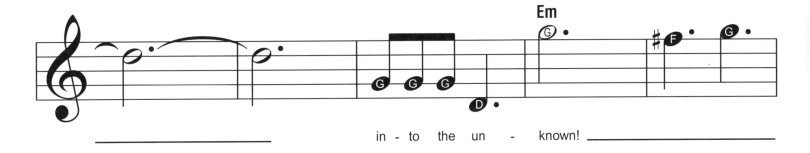

_____ in - to the un - known! _____

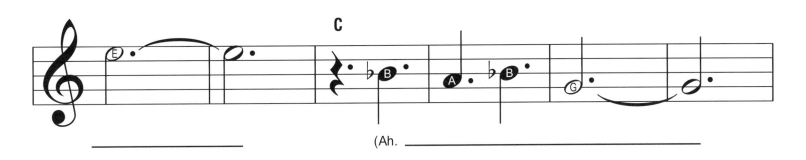

_____ (Ah. _____

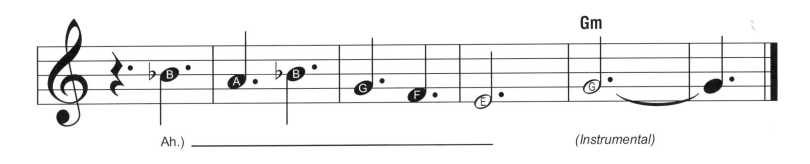

Ah.) _____ (Instrumental)

Let It Go
from FROZEN

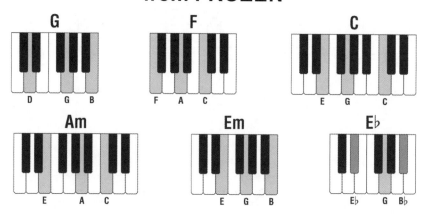

Music and Lyrics by Kristen Anderson-Lopez
and Robert Lopez

Flowing

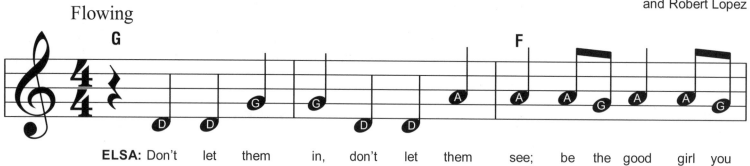

ELSA: Don't let them in, don't let them see; be the good girl you

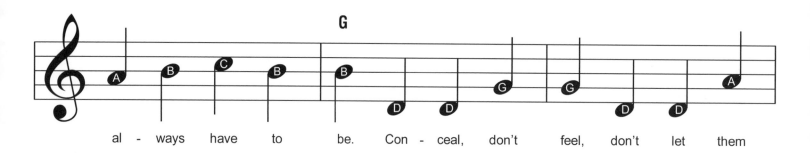

al - ways have to be. Con - ceal, don't feel, don't let them

know... _____   Well, now they know. _____

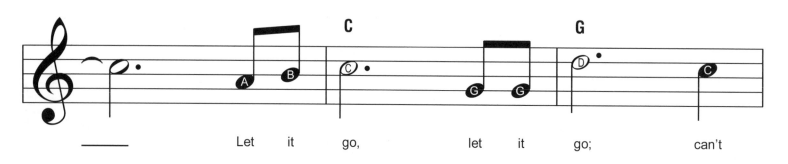

_____   Let it go, let it go; can't

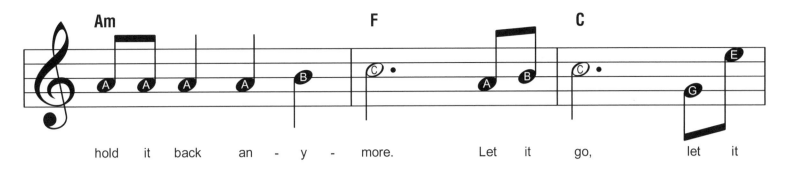

hold it back an - y - more. Let it go, let it

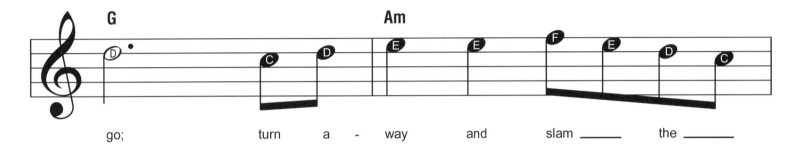

go; turn a - way and slam _____ the _____

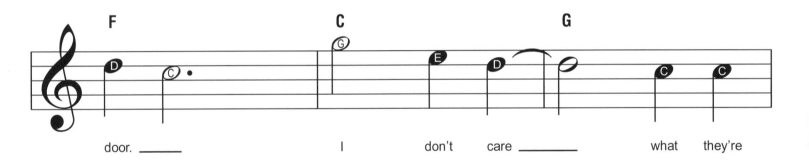

door. _____ I don't care _____ what they're

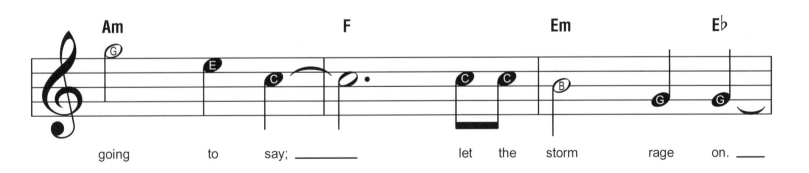

going to say; _____ let the storm rage on. _____

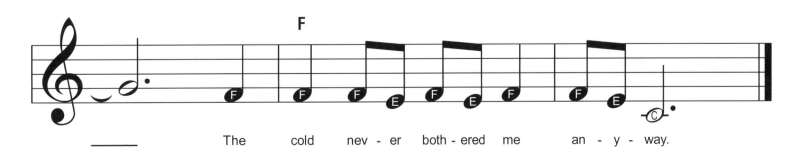

_____ The cold nev - er both - ered me an - y - way.

Level of Concern

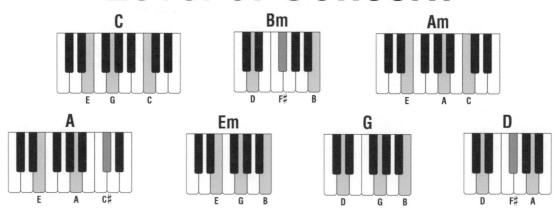

Words and Music by
Tyler Joseph

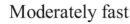

Moderately fast

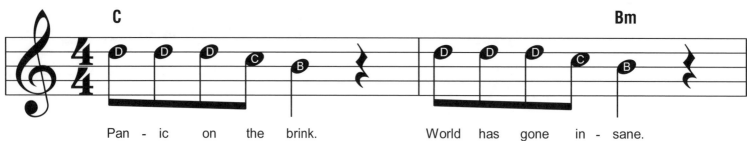

Pan - ic on the brink. World has gone in - sane.

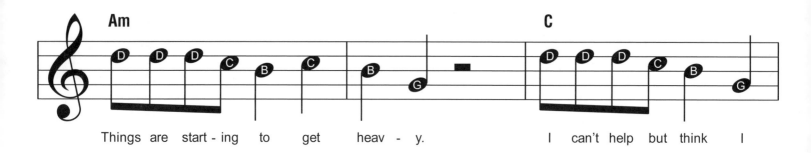

Things are start - ing to get heav - y. I can't help but think I

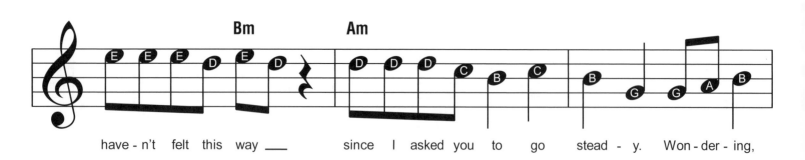

have - n't felt this way ___ since I asked you to go stead - y. Won - der - ing,

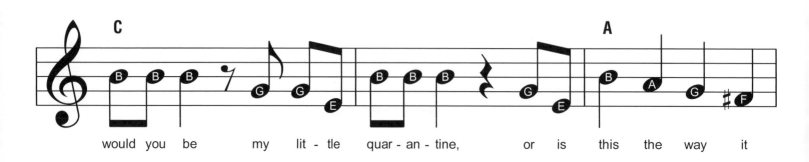

would you be my lit - tle quar - an - tine, or is this the way it

57

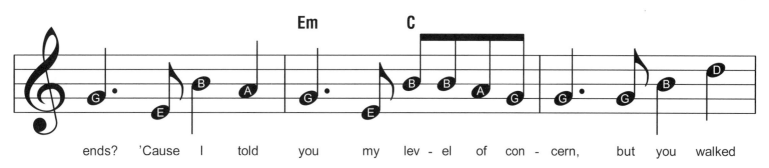

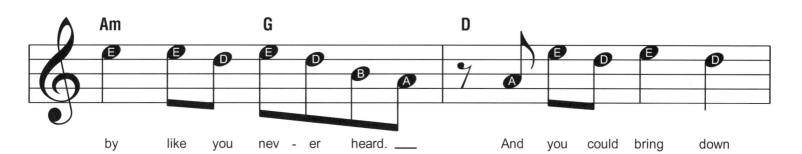

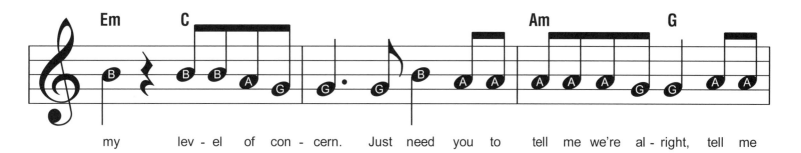

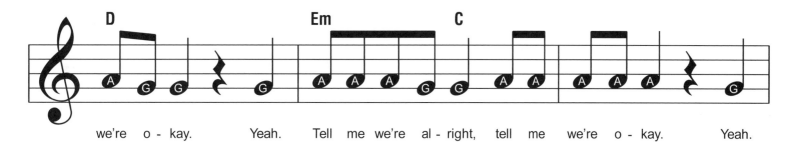

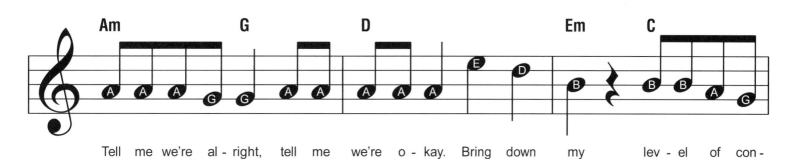

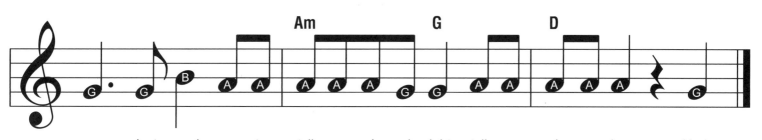

Love Yourself

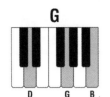 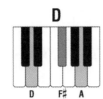 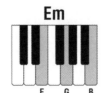 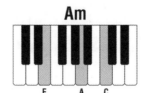 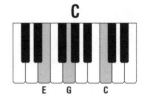

Words and Music by Justin Bieber,
Benjamin Levin, Ed Sheeran,
Joshua Gudwin and Scott Braun

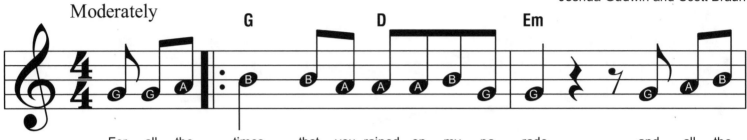

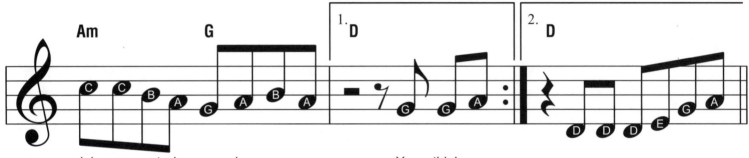

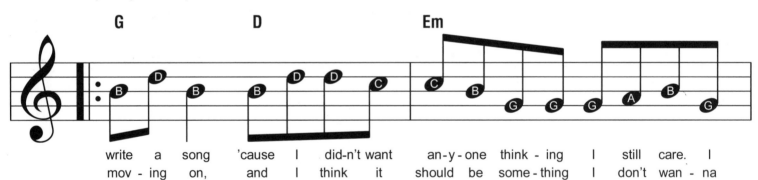

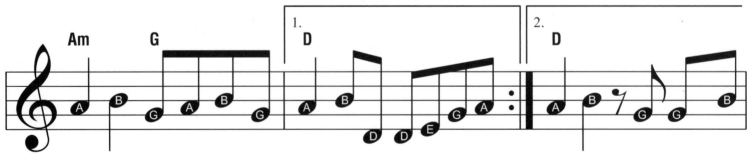

59

The Middle

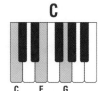 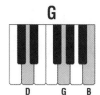 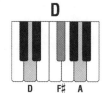 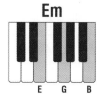

Words and Music by Sarah Aarons,
Marcus Lomax, Jordan Johnson,
Anton Zaslavski, Kyle Trewartha,
Michael Trewartha and Stefan Johnson

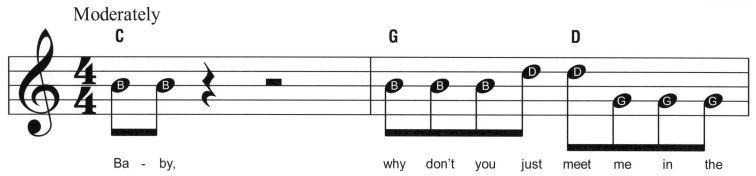

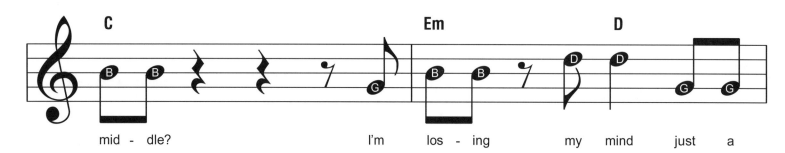

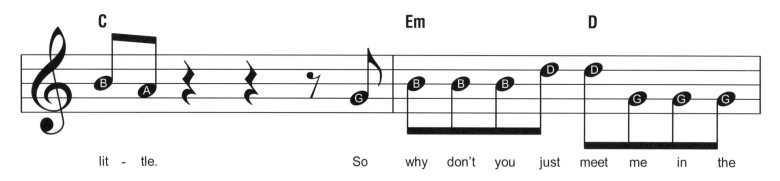

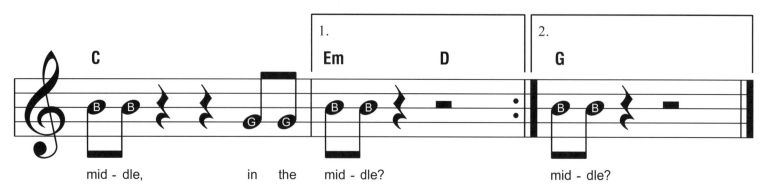

Stereo Hearts

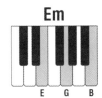 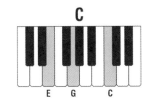 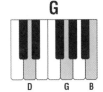 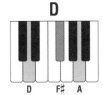

Words and Music by Brandon Lowry,
Dan Omelio, Adam Levine,
Ammar Malik, Benjamin Levin,
Travis McCoy, Disashi Lumumba-Kasongo,
Matthew McGinley and Eric Roberts

Moderately

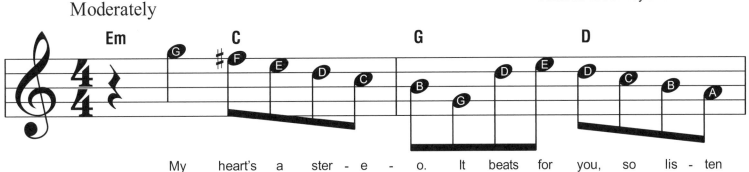

My heart's a ster-e-o. It beats for you, so lis-ten

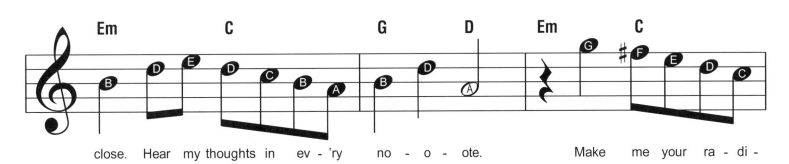

close. Hear my thoughts in ev-'ry no-o-ote. Make me your ra-di-

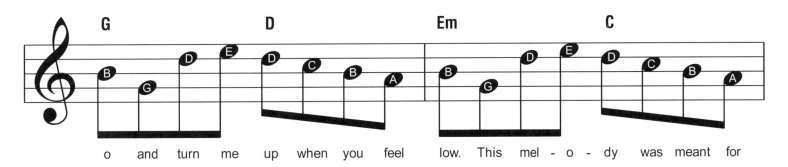

o and turn me up when you feel low. This mel-o-dy was meant for

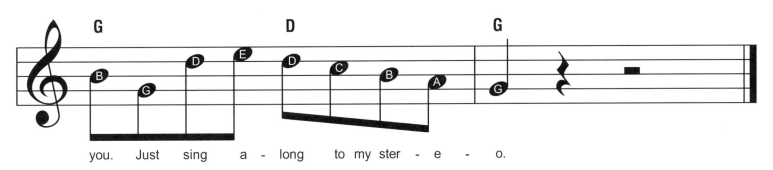

you. Just sing a-long to my ster-e-o.

A Million Dreams
from THE GREATEST SHOWMAN

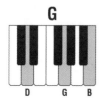
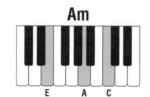
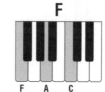
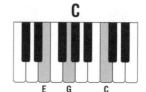

Words and Music by Benj Pasek
and Justin Paul

Moderately

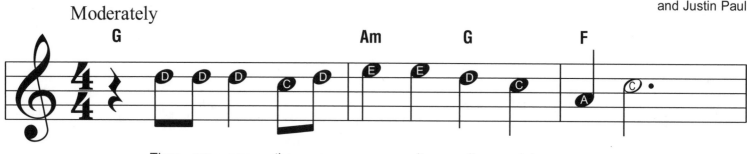

They can say, they can say it all sounds cra - zy

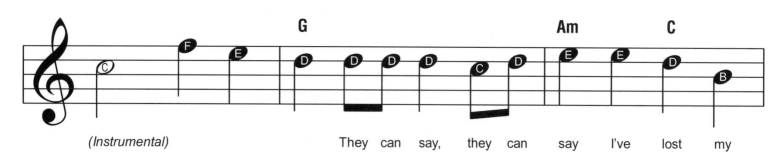

(Instrumental)   They can say, they can say I've lost my

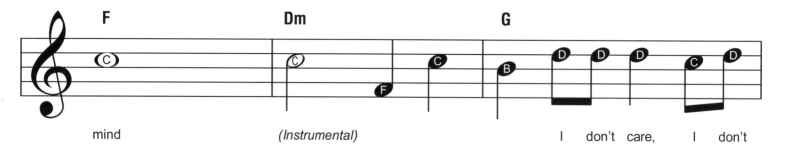

mind   (Instrumental)   I don't care, I don't

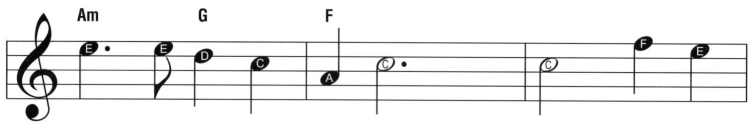

care, so call me cra - zy   (Instrumental)

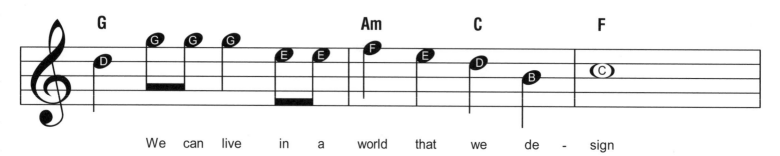

We can live in a world that we de - sign

63

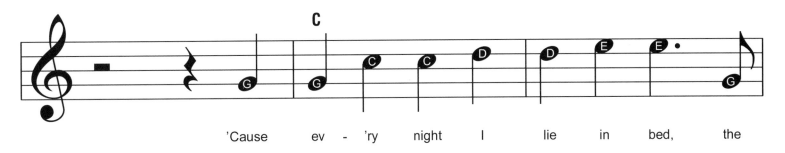

'Cause ev - 'ry night I lie in bed, the

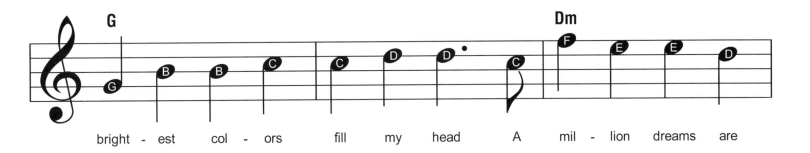

bright - est col - ors fill my head   A mil - lion dreams are

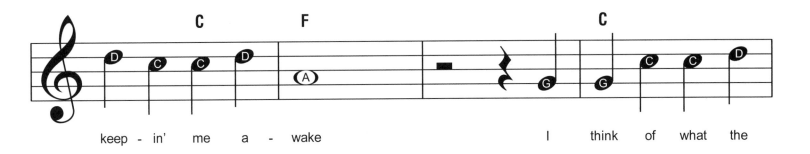

keep - in' me a - wake   I think of what the

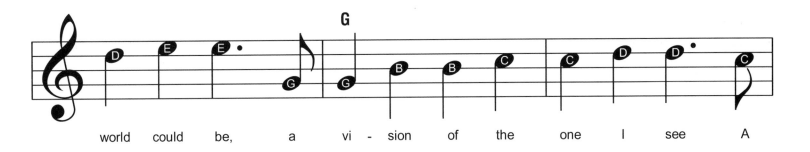

world could be, a vi - sion of the one I see   A

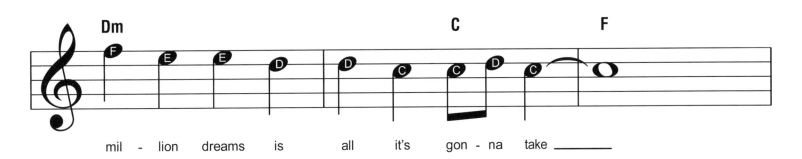

mil - lion dreams is all it's gon - na take _____

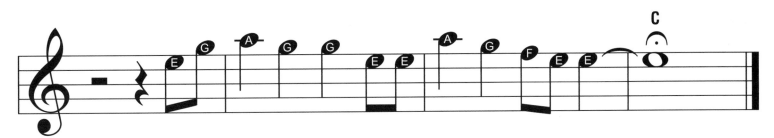

Oh, a mil - lion dreams for the world we're gon - na make _____

Moonlight

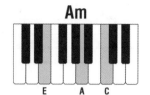
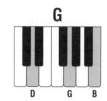
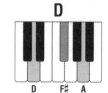
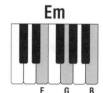
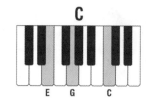

Words and Music by Grace VanderWaal
and Ido Zmishlany

Moderate half-time feel

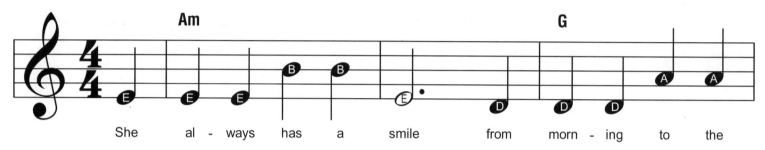

She al - ways has a smile from morn - ing to the

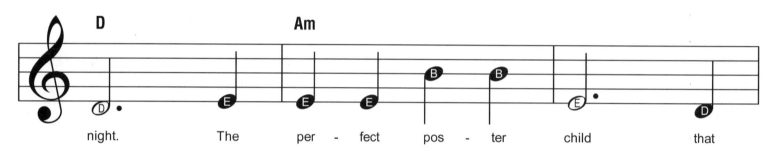

night. The per - fect pos - ter child that

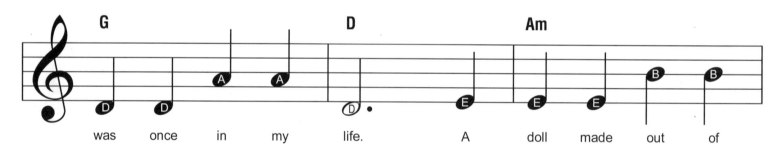

was once in my life. A doll made out of

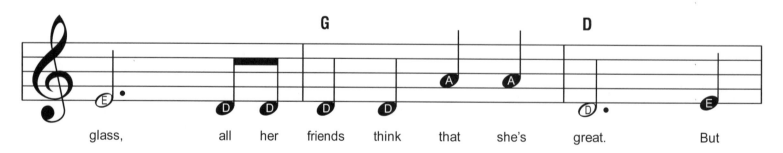

glass, all her friends think that she's great. But

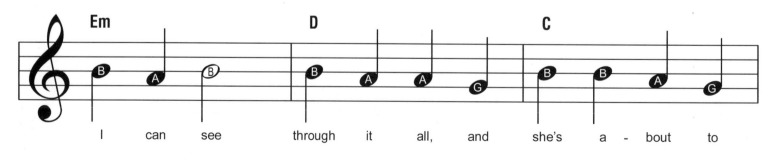

I can see through it all, and she's a - bout to

No Tears Left to Cry

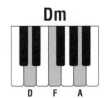
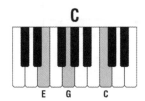
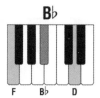
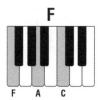

Words and Music by Ariana Grande,
Savan Kotecha, Max Martin
and Ilya

Moderately fast

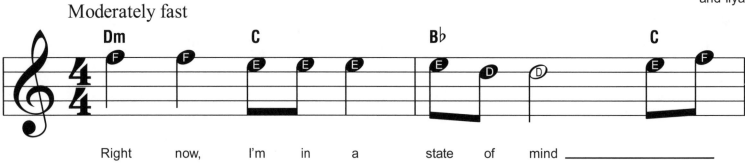

Right now, I'm in a state of mind _____

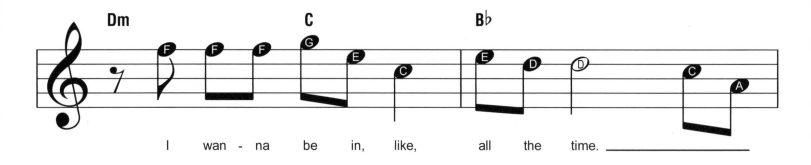

I wan - na be in, like, all the time. _____

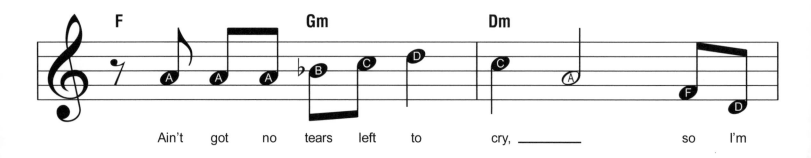

Ain't got no tears left to cry, _____ so I'm

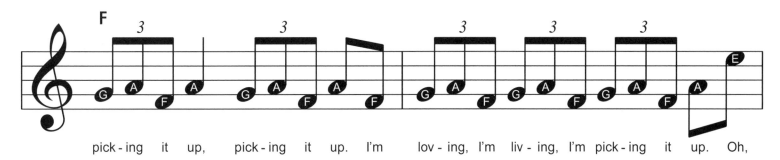

picking it up, picking it up. I'm loving, I'm living, I'm picking it up. Oh,

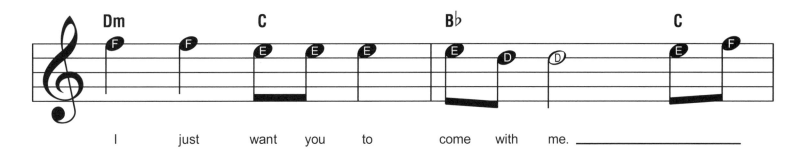

I just want you to come with me. _____

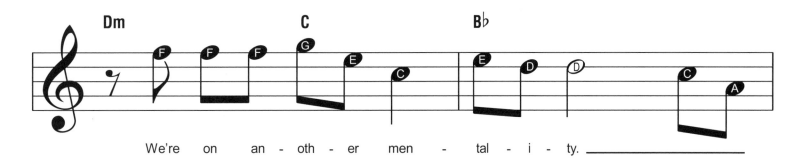

We're on another mentality. _____

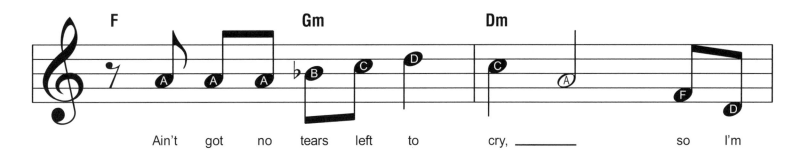

Ain't got no tears left to cry, _____ so I'm

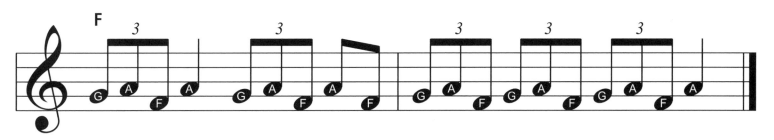

picking it up, picking it up. I'm loving, I'm living, I'm picking it up.

Ocean Eyes

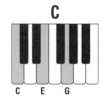
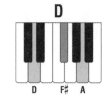
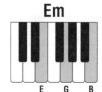
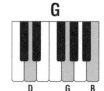

Words and Music by
Finneas O'Connell

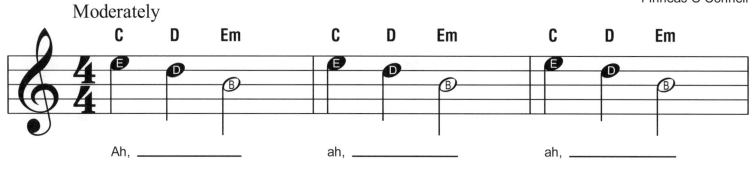

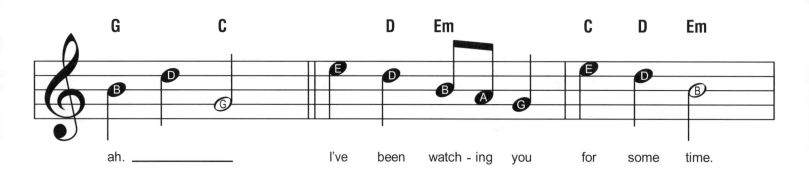

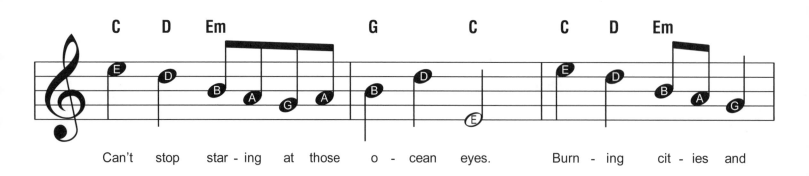

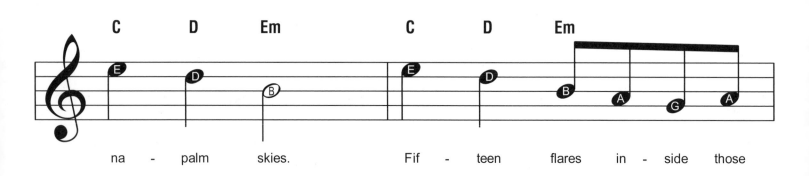

69

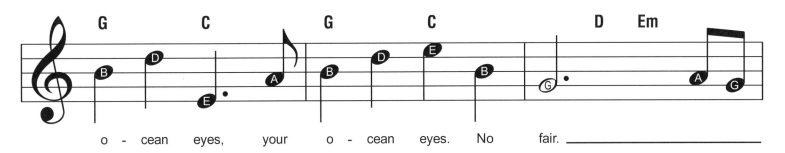

o - cean eyes, your o - cean eyes. No fair. _____

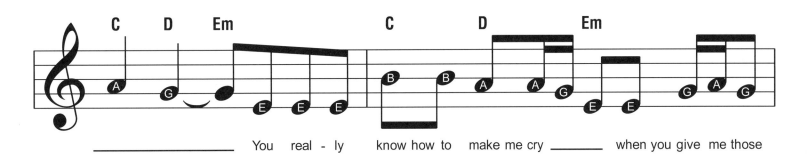

_____ You real - ly know how to make me cry _____ when you give me those

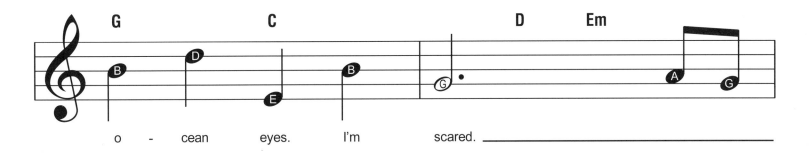

o - cean eyes. I'm scared. _____

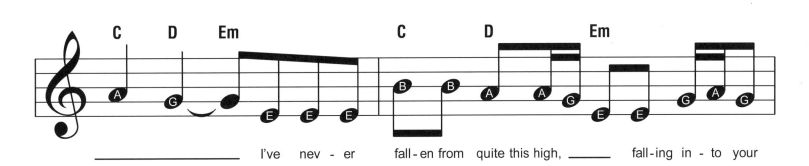

_____ I've nev - er fall - en from quite this high, _____ fall - ing in - to your

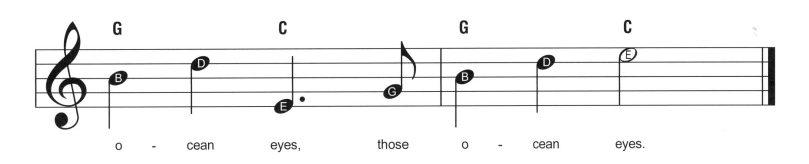

o - cean eyes, those o - cean eyes.

Old Town Road
(Remix)

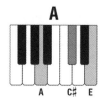
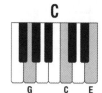

Words and Music by Trent Reznor,
Billy Ray Cyrus, Jocelyn Donald,
Atticus Ross, Kiowa Roukema
and Montero Lamar Hill

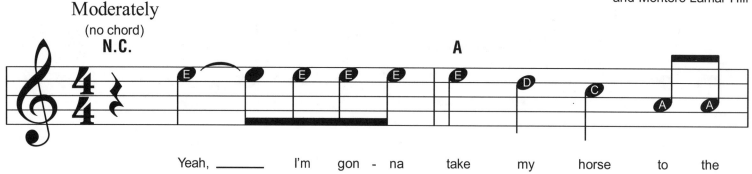

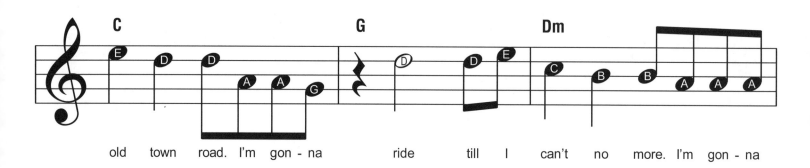

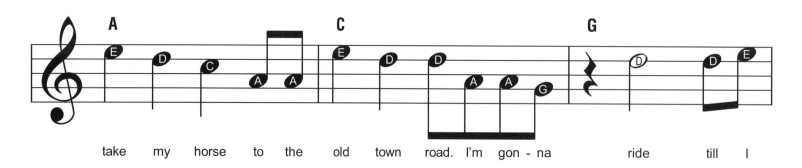

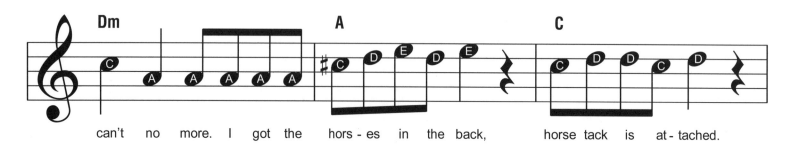

One Call Away

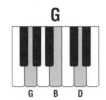
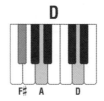
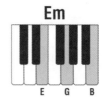
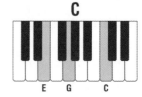

Words and Music by Charlie Puth,
Justin Franks, Breyan Isaac,
Matt Prime, Blake Anthony Carter
and Maureen McDonald

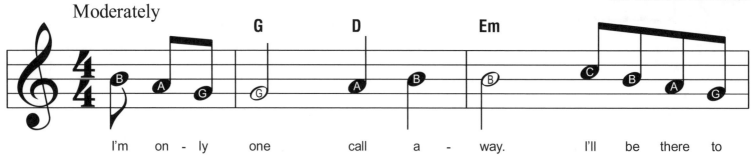

I'm on - ly one call a - way. I'll be there to

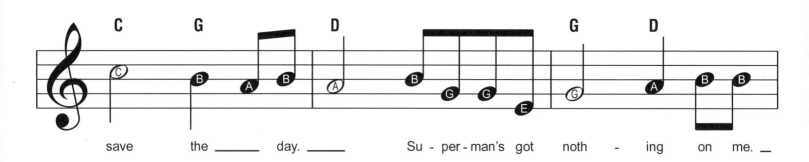

save the _____ day. _____ Su - per - man's got noth - ing on me. _

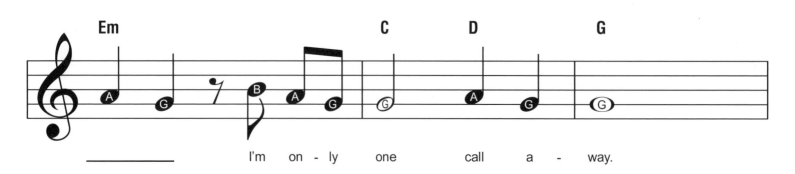

_____ I'm on - ly one call a - way.

73

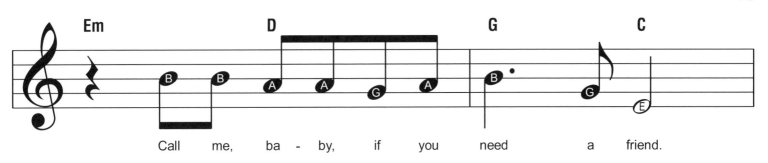

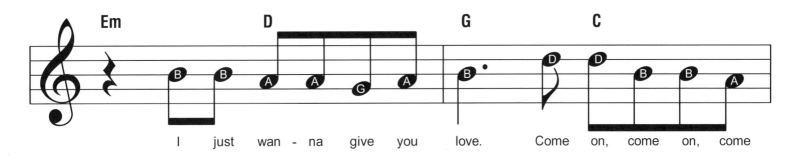

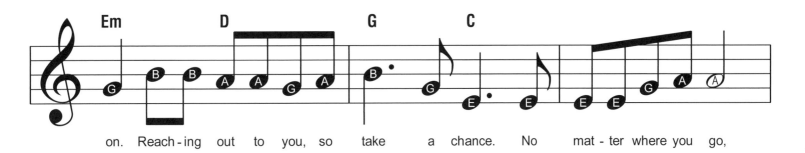

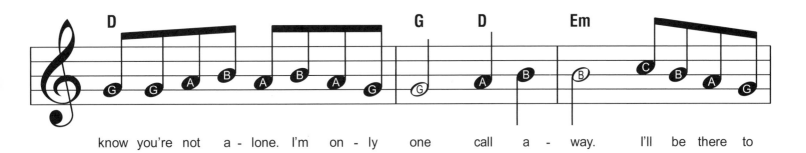

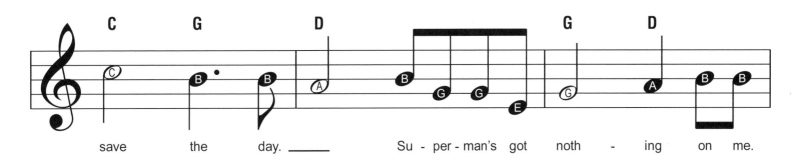

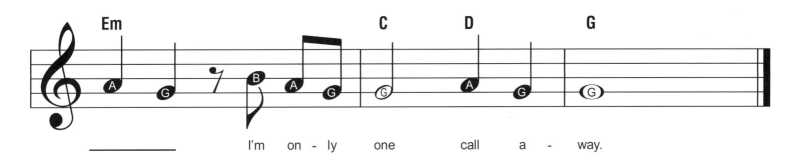

100 Years

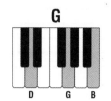 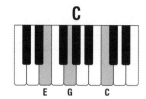 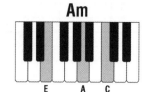 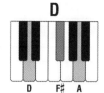 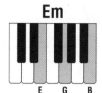

Words and Music by
John Ondrasik

Moderately fast

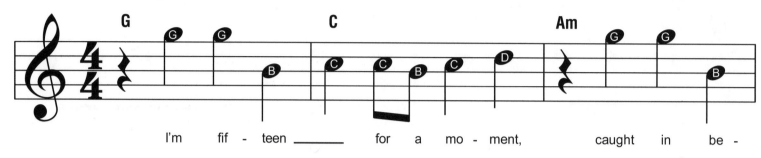

I'm fif - teen _____ for a mo - ment, caught in be -

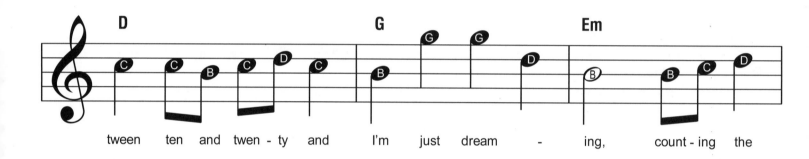

tween ten and twen - ty and I'm just dream - ing, count - ing the

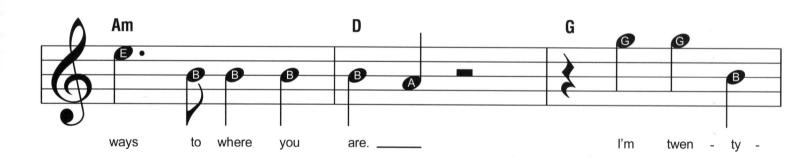

ways to where you are. _____ I'm twen - ty -

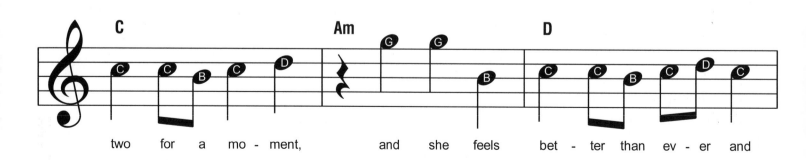

two for a mo - ment, and she feels bet - ter than ev - er and

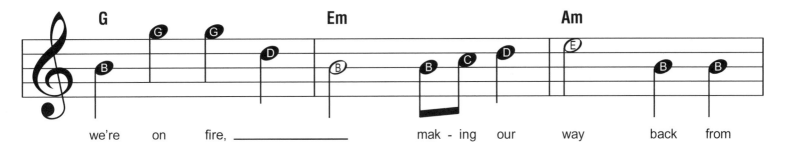

we're on fire, _____ mak - ing our way back from

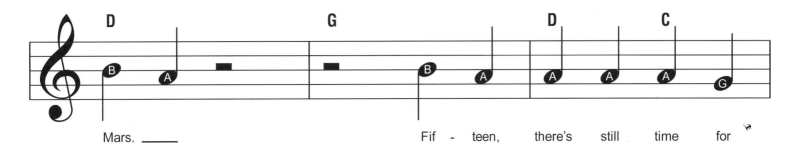

Mars. ____ Fif - teen, there's still time for

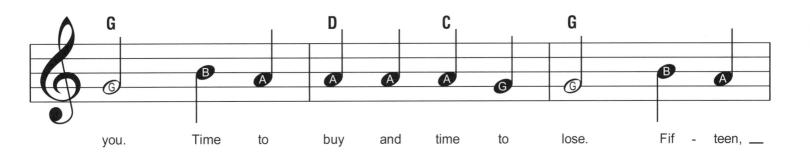

you. Time to buy and time to lose. Fif - teen, __

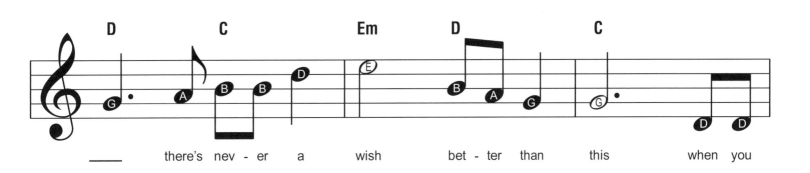

__ there's nev - er a wish bet - ter than this when you

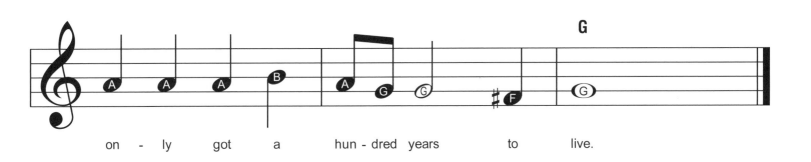

on - ly got a hun - dred years to live.

Pompeii

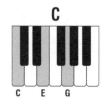 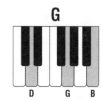 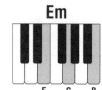 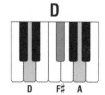

Words and Music by
Dan Smith

Moderately fast

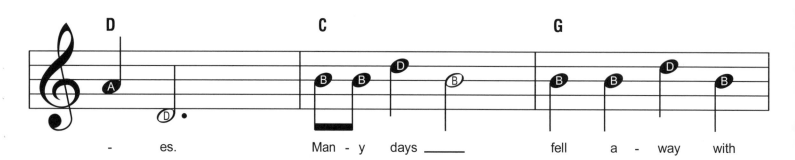

I was left to my own _____ de - vic -

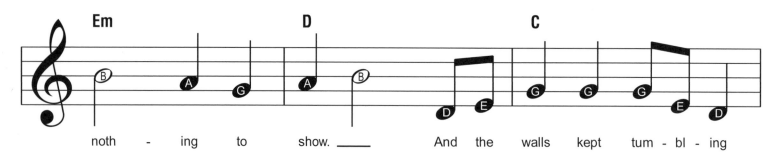

- es. Man - y days _____ fell a - way with

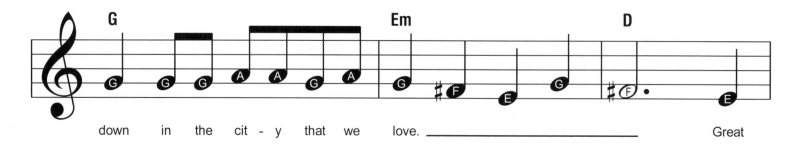

noth - ing to show. _____ And the walls kept tum - bl - ing

down in the cit - y that we love. _____ Great

clouds roll o - ver the hills, bring - ing dark - ness from a - bove. _____

Roar

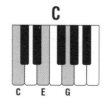 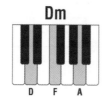 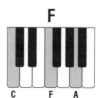

Words and Music by Katy Perry,
Max Martin, Dr. Luke,
Bonnie McKee and Henry Walter

Quickly

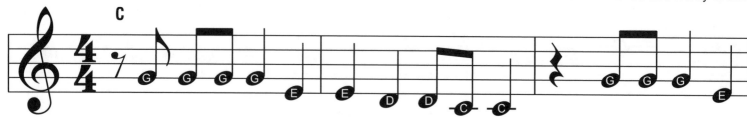

I used to bite my tongue and hold my breath, scared to rock the
I guess that I for - got I had a choice. I let you push me

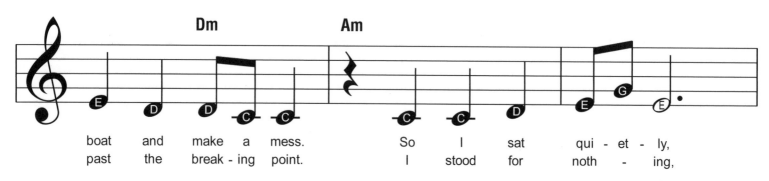

boat and make a mess. So I sat qui - et - ly,
past the break - ing point. I stood for noth - ing,

a - greed po - lite - ly.
so I fell for ev - 'ry - thing. You

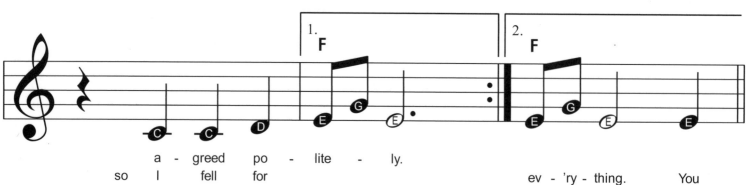

held me down, but I got up, al - read - y brush - ing
held me down, but I got up. Get read - y 'cause I've

79

Rude

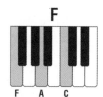 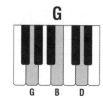 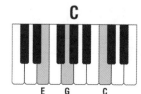 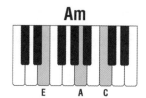

Words and Music by Nasri Atweh,
Mark Pellizzer, Alex Tanas,
Ben Spivak and Adam Messinger

Moderate Reggae

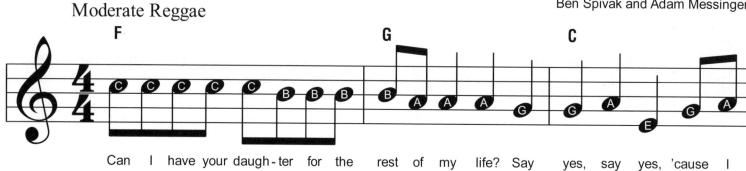

Can I have your daugh-ter for the rest of my life? Say yes, say yes, 'cause I

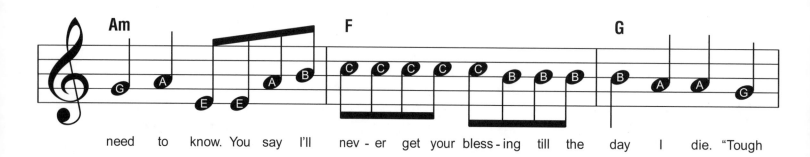

need to know. You say I'll nev-er get your bless-ing till the day I die. "Tough

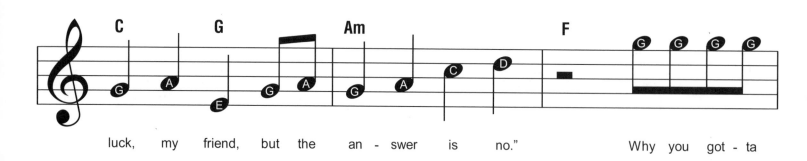

luck, my friend, but the an-swer is no." Why you got-ta

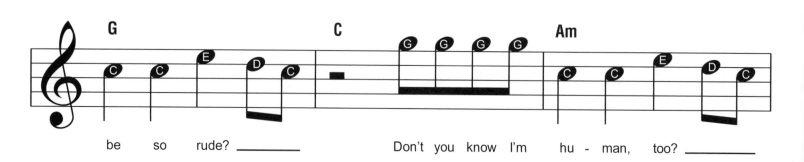

be so rude? _____ Don't you know I'm hu-man, too? _____

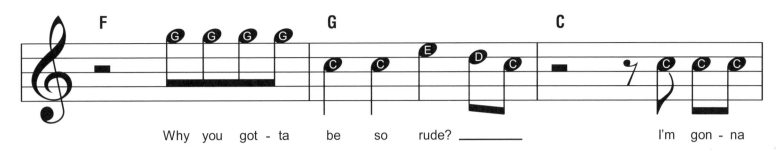

Why you got - ta be so rude? _____ I'm gon - na

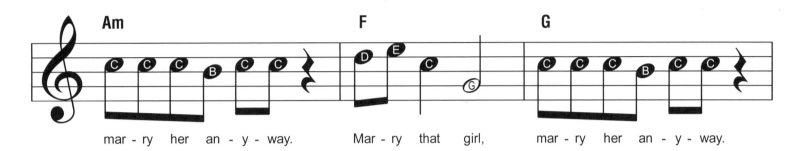

mar - ry her an - y - way. Mar - ry that girl, mar - ry her an - y - way.

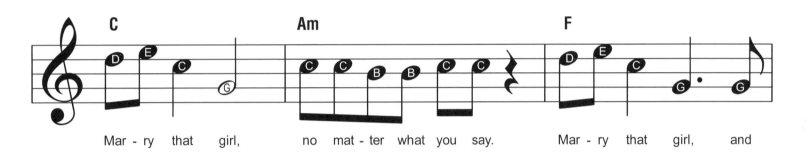

Mar - ry that girl, no mat - ter what you say. Mar - ry that girl, and

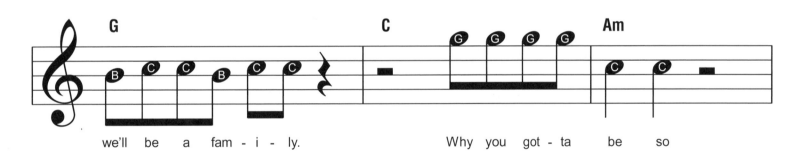

we'll be a fam - i - ly. Why you got - ta be so

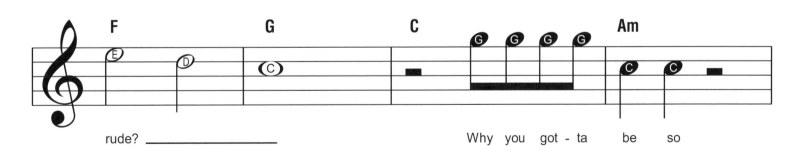

rude? _____ Why you got - ta be so

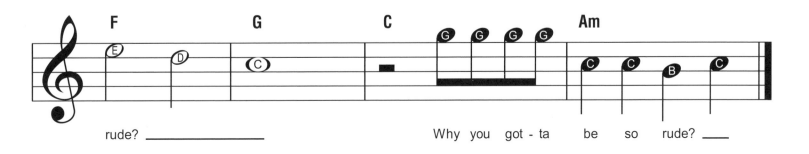

rude? _____ Why you got - ta be so rude? ____

Safe and Sound

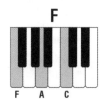 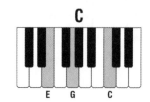 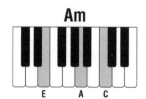 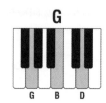

Words and Music by Ryan Takacs Merchant
and Sebouh (Sebu) Simonian

Dance Pop

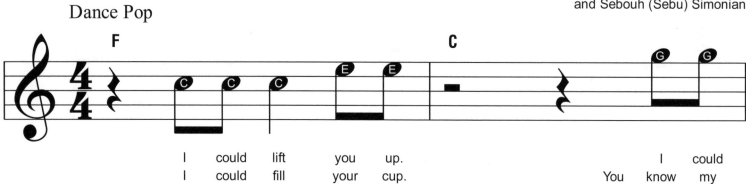

I could lift you up. I could
I could fill your cup. You know my

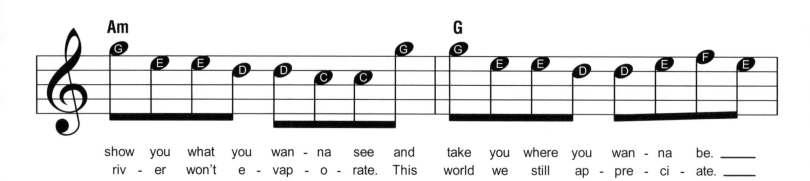

show you what you wan - na see and take you where you wan - na be. _____
riv - er won't e - vap - o - rate. This world we still ap - pre - ci - ate. _____

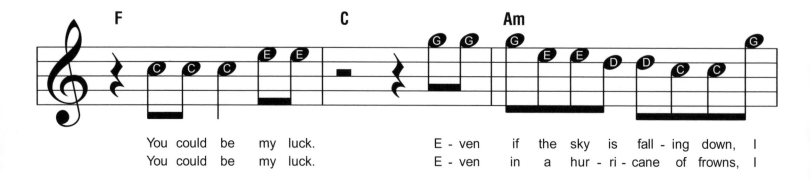

You could be my luck. E - ven if the sky is fall - ing down, I
You could be my luck. E - ven in a hur - ri - cane of frowns, I

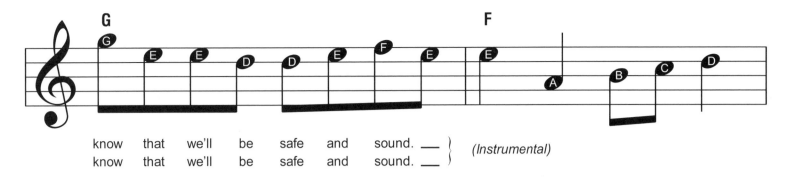

know that we'll be safe and sound. ___ } (Instrumental)
know that we'll be safe and sound. ___

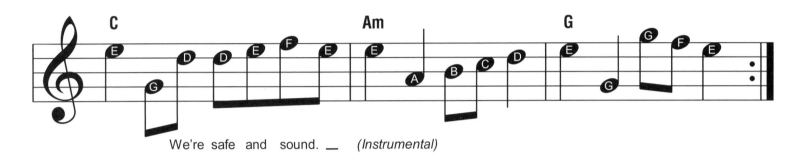

We're safe and sound. ___ (Instrumental)

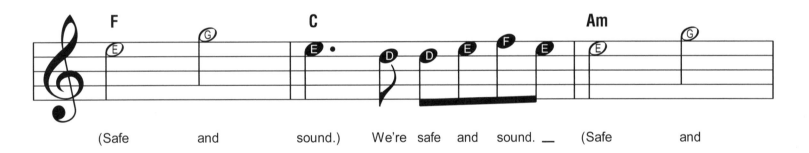

(Safe and sound.) We're safe and sound. ___ (Safe and

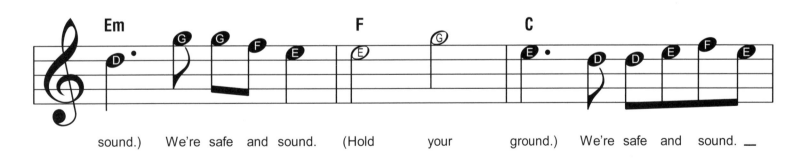

sound.) We're safe and sound. (Hold your ground.) We're safe and sound. ___

(Safe and sound.) We're safe and sound.

Scars to Your Beautiful

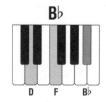 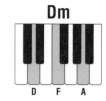 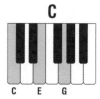

Words and Music by Alessia Caracciolo,
Warren Felder, Coleridge Tillman
and Andrew Wansel

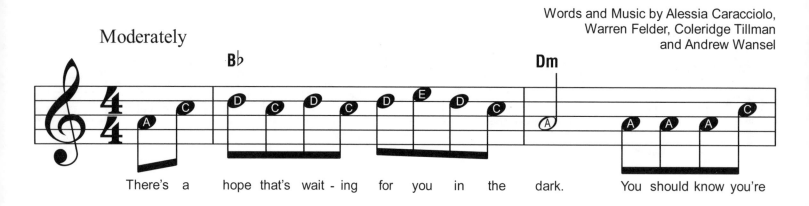

There's a hope that's wait-ing for you in the dark. You should know you're

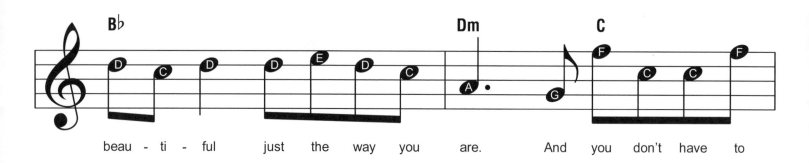

beau-ti-ful just the way you are. And you don't have to

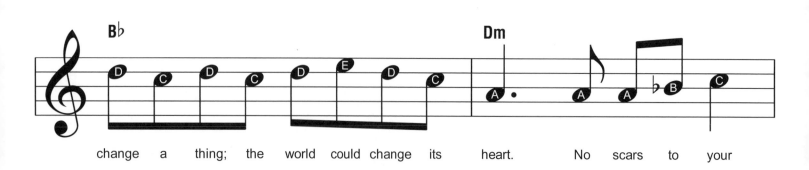

change a thing; the world could change its heart. No scars to your

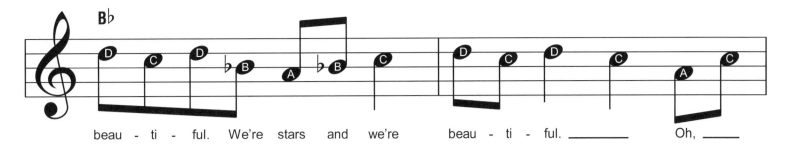

beau - ti - ful. We're stars and we're beau - ti - ful. _____ Oh, _____

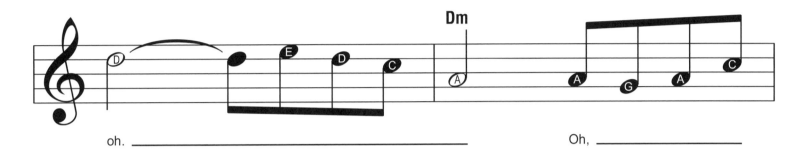

oh. _____ Oh, _____

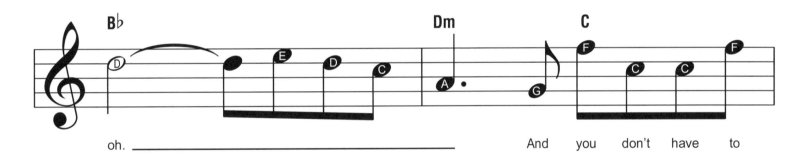

oh. _____ And you don't have to

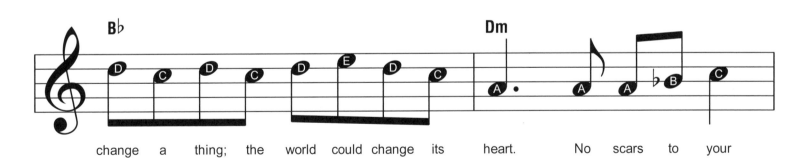

change a thing; the world could change its heart. No scars to your

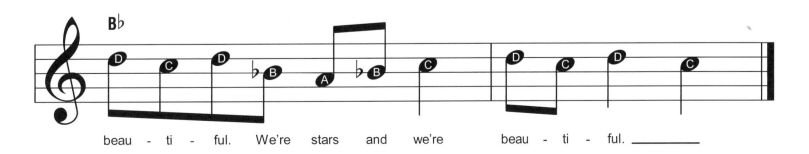

beau - ti - ful. We're stars and we're beau - ti - ful. _____

Shake It Off

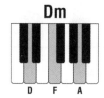 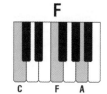 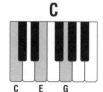

Words and Music by Taylor Swift,
Max Martin and Shellback

Moderately fast

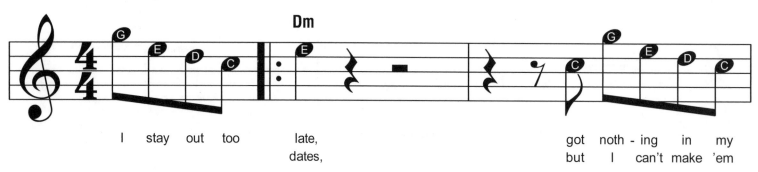

I stay out too late,   got noth-ing in my
dates,   but I can't make 'em

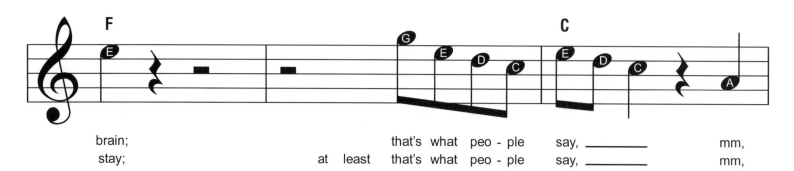

brain;   that's what peo-ple say, _____ mm,
stay;   at least that's what peo-ple say, _____ mm,

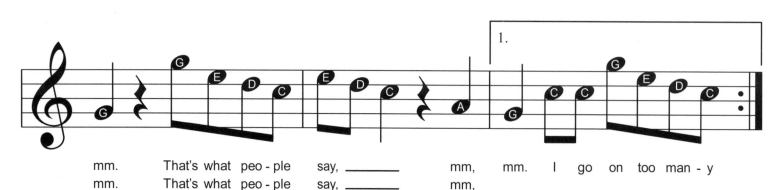

1.

mm. That's what peo-ple say, _____ mm, mm. I go on too man-y
mm. That's what peo-ple say, _____ mm,

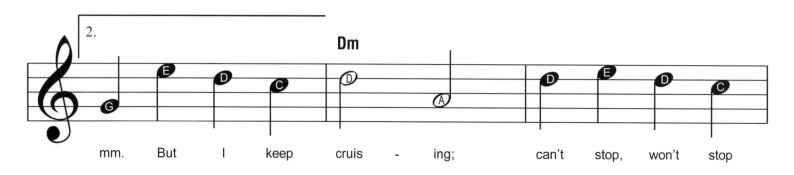

2.

mm. But I keep cruis-ing;   can't stop, won't stop

Shut Up and Dance

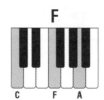 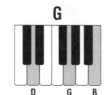  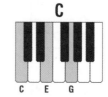

Words and Music by Ryan McMahon,
Ben Berger, Sean Waugaman,
Eli Maiman, Nicholas Petricca
and Kevin Ray

Moderate Rock

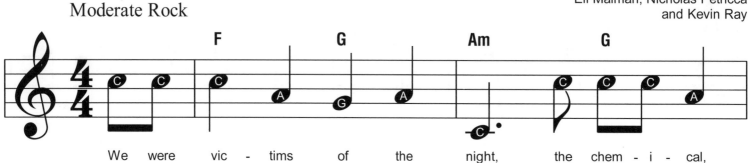

We were vic-tims of the night, the chem-i-cal,

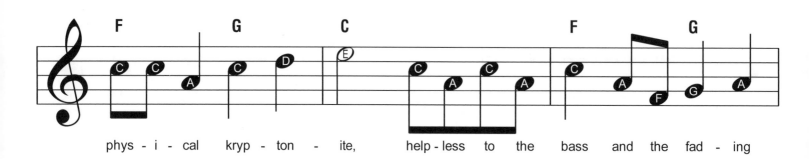

phys-i-cal kryp-ton-ite, help-less to the bass and the fad-ing

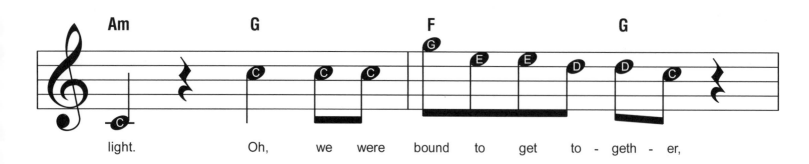

light. Oh, we were bound to get to-geth-er,

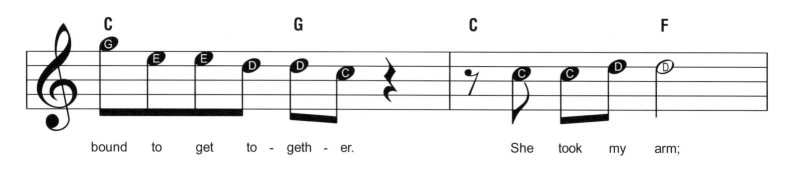

bound to get to-geth-er. She took my arm;

Something Just Like This

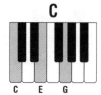
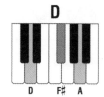
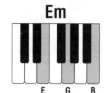

Words and Music by Andrew Taggart,
Chris Martin, Guy Berryman,
Jonny Buckland and Will Champion

Moderately
(no chord)

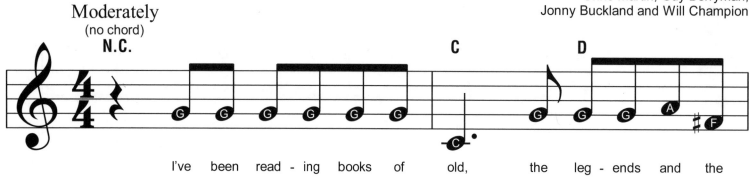

I've been read - ing books of old, the leg - ends and the

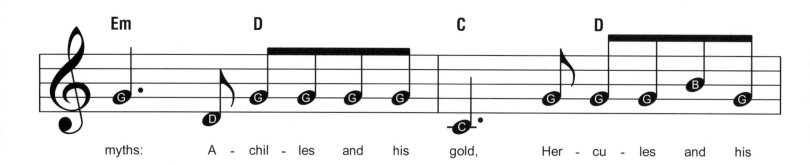

myths: A - chil - les and his gold, Her - cu - les and his

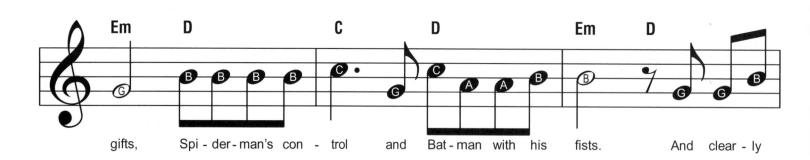

gifts, Spi - der - man's con - trol and Bat - man with his fists. And clear - ly

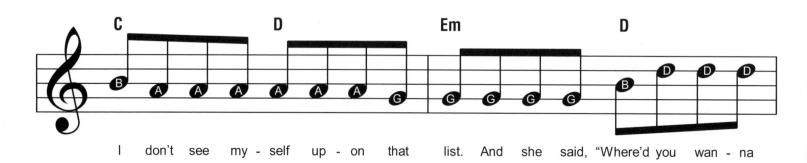

I don't see my - self up - on that list. And she said, "Where'd you wan - na

Spirit
from THE LION KING 2019

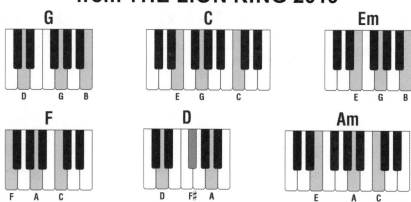

Written by Timothy McKenzie,
Ilya Salmanzadeh and Beyoncé

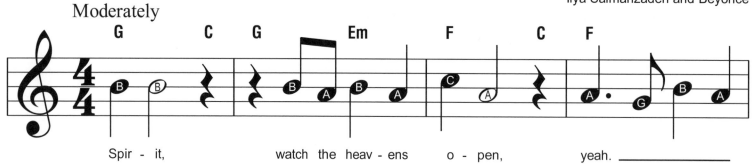

Spir - it,   watch the heav - ens   o - pen,   yeah. _____

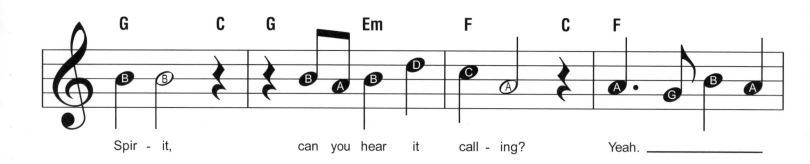

Spir - it,   can you hear   it   call - ing?   Yeah. _____

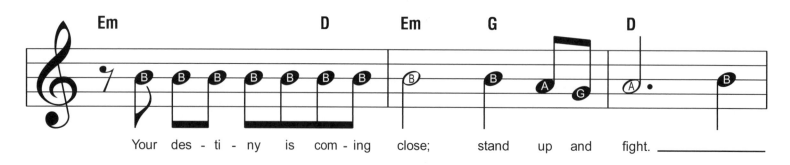

Your des - ti - ny   is   com - ing   close;   stand   up   and   fight. _____

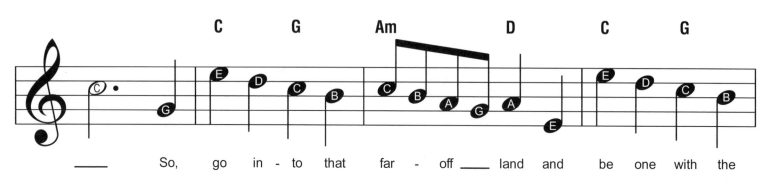

_____ So,   go   in - to   that   far - off _____ land   and   be   one   with   the

Story of My Life

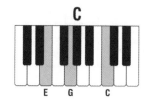
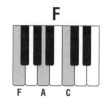
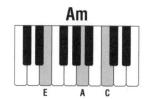

Words and Music by Jamie Scott,
John Henry Ryan, Julian Bunetta,
Harry Styles, Liam Payne,
Louis Tomlinson, Niall Horan
and Zain Malik

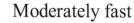
Moderately fast

The sto - ry of my life: I take her home. I

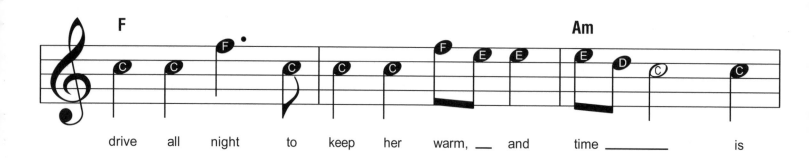

drive all night to keep her warm, ___ and time ___ is

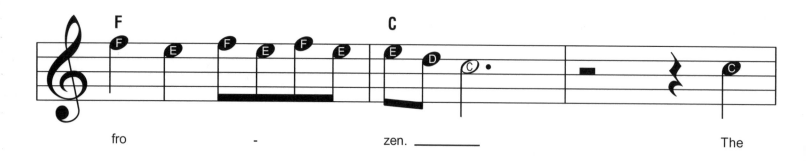

fro - zen. ___ The

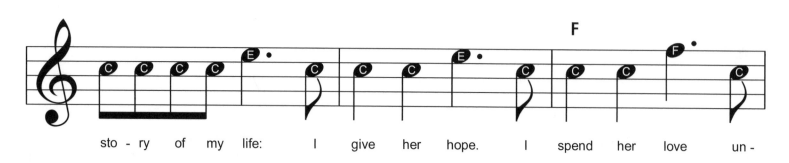

sto - ry of my life: I give her hope. I spend her love un -

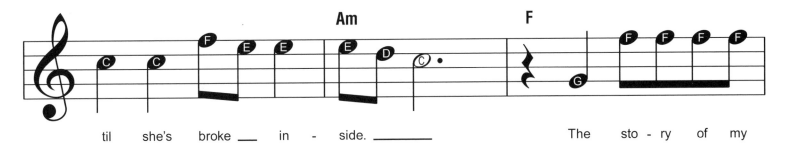

til she's broke ___ in - side. _____ The sto - ry of my

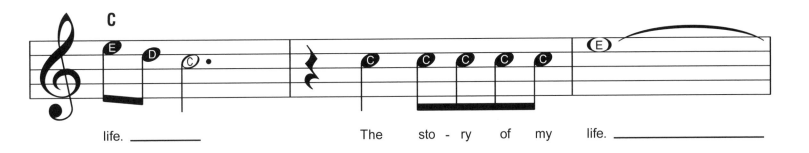

life. _____ The sto - ry of my life. _____

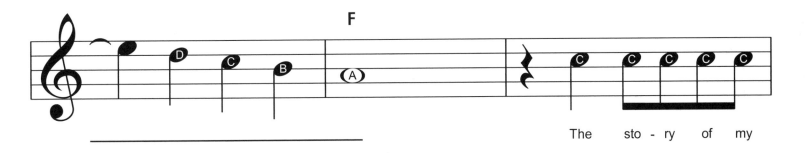

_____ The sto - ry of my

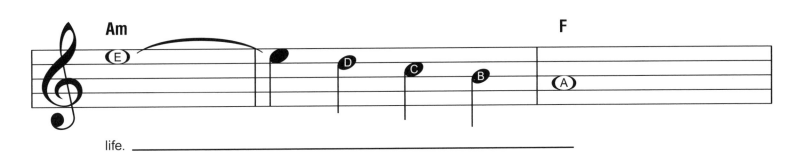

life. _____

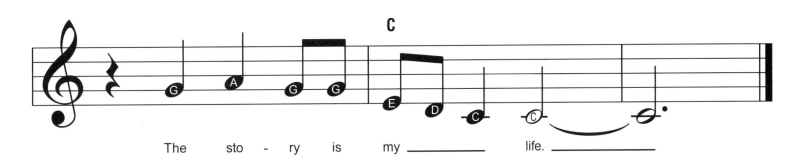

The sto - ry is my _____ life. _____

Stressed Out

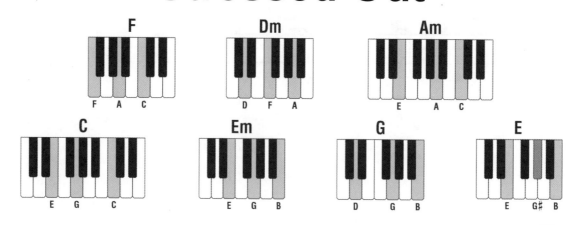

Words and Music by
Tyler Joseph

Half-time Shuffle

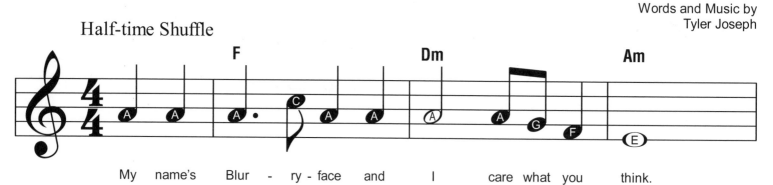

My name's Blur - ry - face and I care what you think.

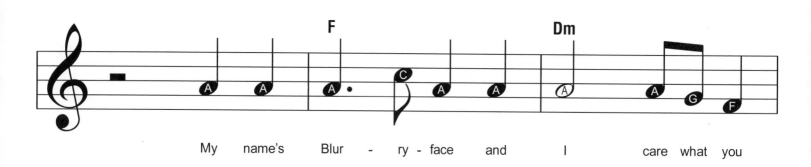

My name's Blur - ry - face and I care what you

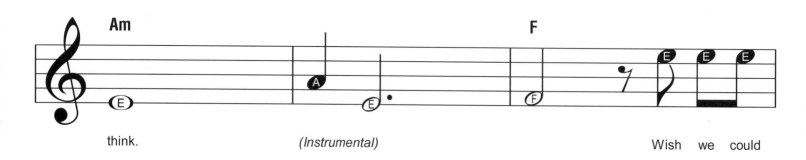

think.   (Instrumental)   Wish we could

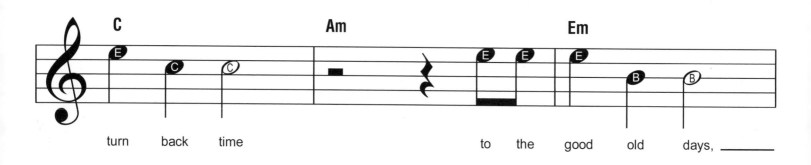

turn back time   to the good old days, _____

Stronger
(What Doesn't Kill You)

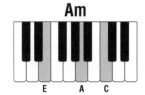
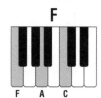
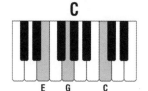
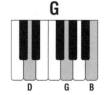

Words and Music by Greg Kurstin,
Alexandra Tamposi, David Gamson
and Jorgen Elofsson

Dance Pop

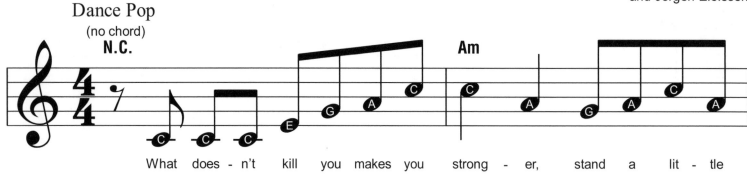

What does-n't kill you makes you strong - er, stand a lit - tle

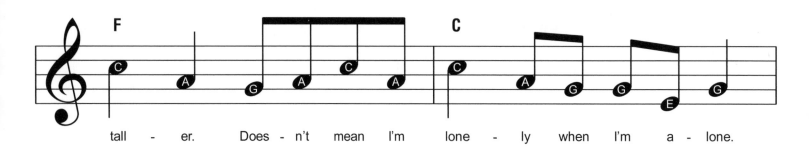

tall - er. Does - n't mean I'm lone - ly when I'm a - lone.

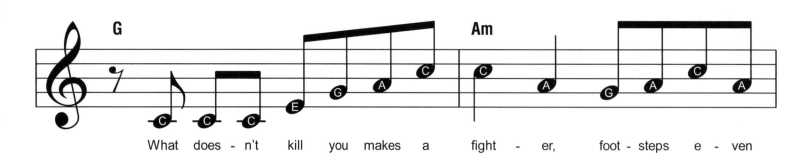

What does - n't kill you makes a fight - er, foot - steps e - ven

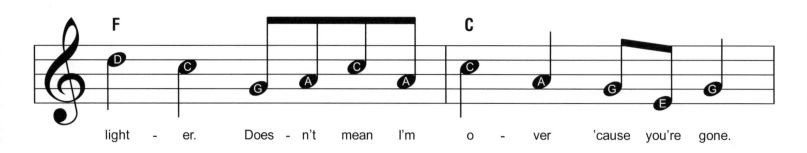

light - er. Does - n't mean I'm o - ver 'cause you're gone.

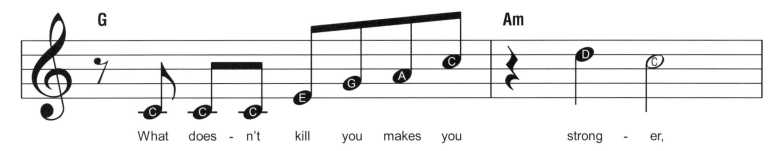

What does - n't kill you makes you strong - er,

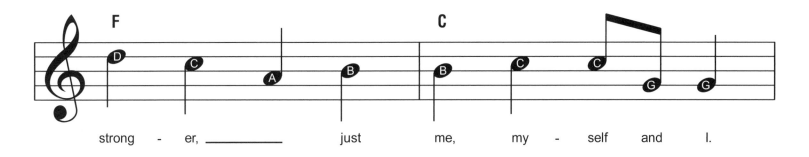

strong - er, _____ just me, my - self and I.

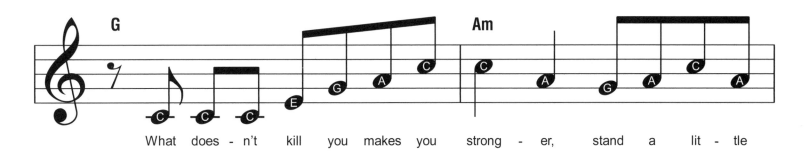

What does - n't kill you makes you strong - er, stand a lit - tle

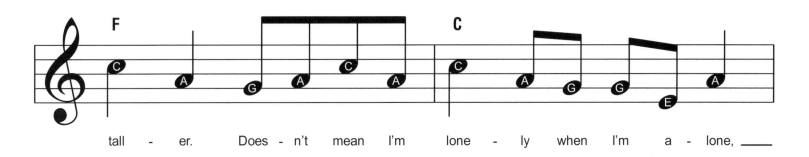

tall - er. Does - n't mean I'm lone - ly when I'm a - lone, ____

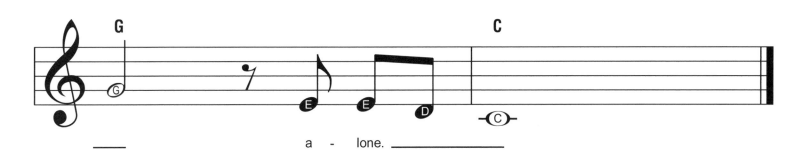

____ a - lone. _____

Sucker

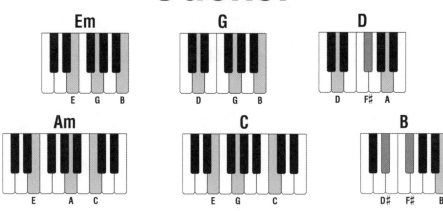

Words and Music by Nick Jonas,
Joseph Jonas, Miles Ale, Mustafa Ahmed,
Ryan Tedder, Louis Bell, Adam Feeney,
Kevin Jonas and Homer Steinweiss

Upbeat Pop

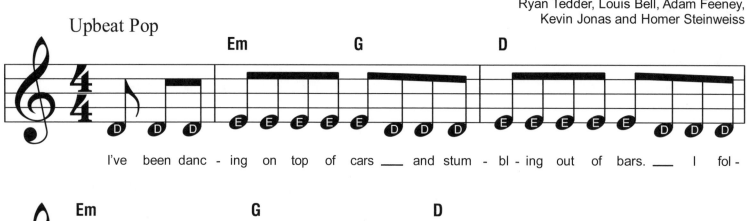

I've been danc - ing on top of cars ___ and stum - bl - ing out of bars. ___ I fol -

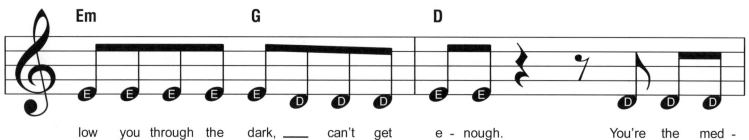

low you through the dark, ___ can't get e - nough. You're the med -

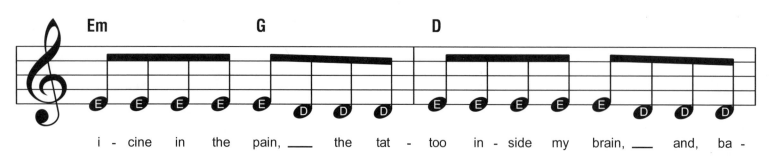

i - cine in the pain, ___ the tat - too in - side my brain, ___ and, ba -

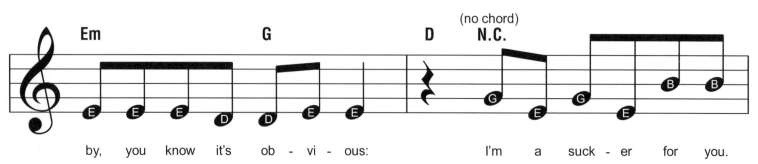

by, you know it's ob - vi - ous: I'm a suck - er for you.

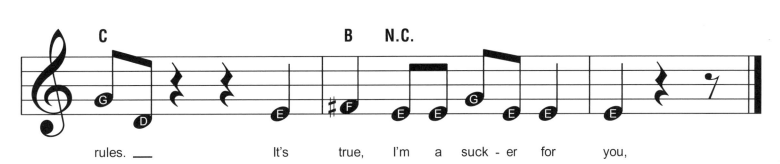

Sunday Best

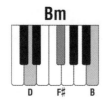
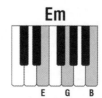
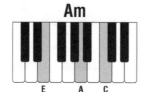
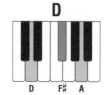

Words and Music by Forrest Frank
and Colin Padalecki

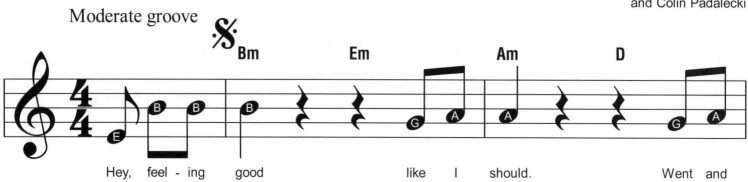

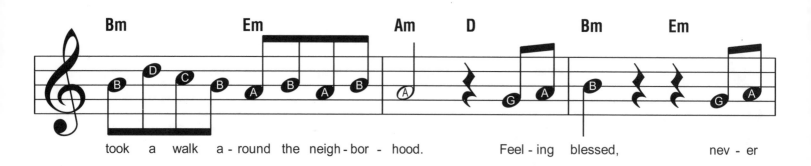

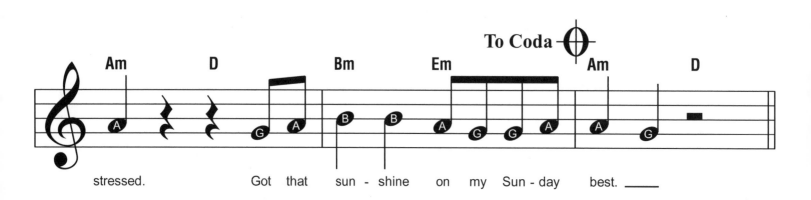

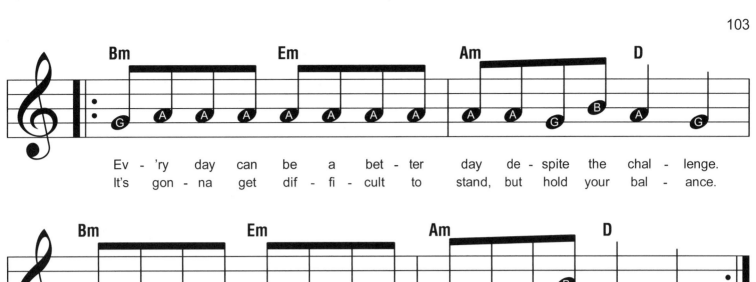

Ev - 'ry day can be a bet - ter day de - spite the chal - lenge.
It's gon - na get dif - fi - cult to stand, but hold your bal - ance.

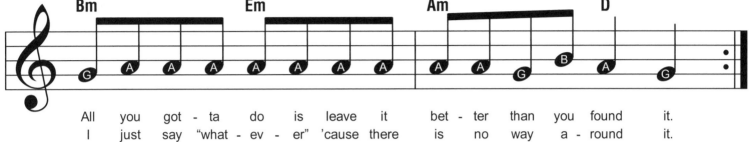

All you got - ta do is leave it bet - ter than you found it.
I just say "what - ev - er" 'cause there is no way a - round it.

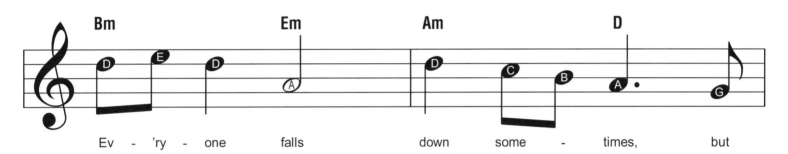

Ev - 'ry - one falls down some - times, but

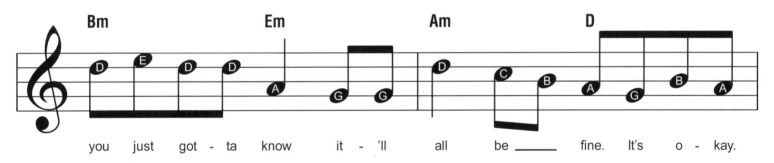

you just got - ta know it - 'll all be _____ fine. It's o - kay.

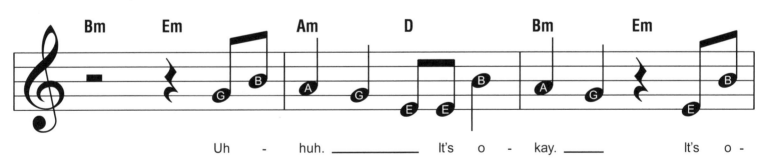

Uh - huh. _____ It's o - kay. _____ It's o -

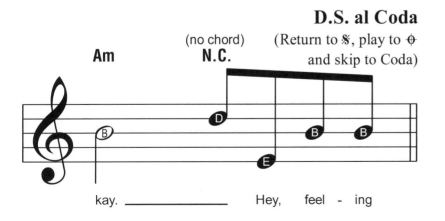

kay. _____ Hey, feel - ing

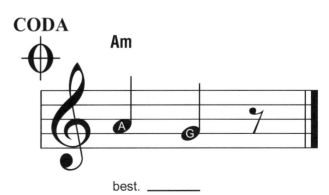

best. _____

Sunflower

from SPIDER-MAN: INTO THE SPIDER-VERSE

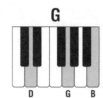
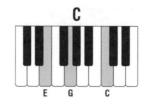
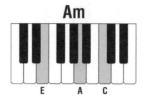

Words and Music by Austin Richard Post,
Carl Austin Rosen, Khalif Brown,
Carter Lang, Louis Bell
and Billy Walsh

Moderately

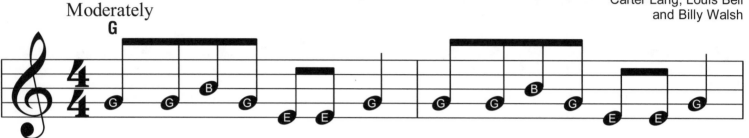

Need-less to say, I keep her in check. She was all bad - bad, nev-er-the-less.

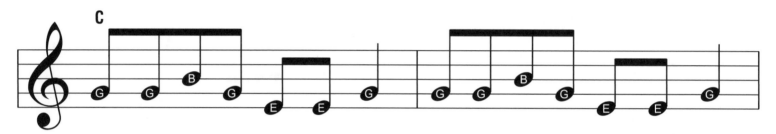

Call-ing it quits now, ba-by, I'm a wreck. Crash at my place, ba-by, you're a wreck.

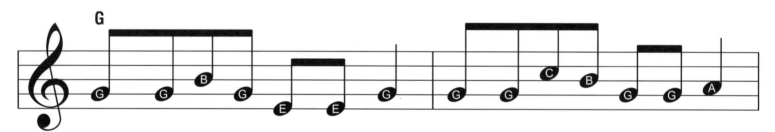

Need-less to say, I'm keep-ing her in check. She was all bad - bad, nev-er-the-less.

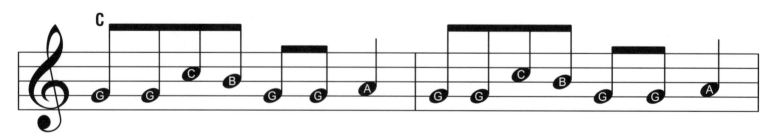

Call-ing it quits now, ba-by, I'm a wreck. Crash at my place, ba-by, you're a wreck.

Superheroes

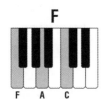 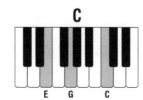 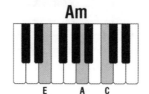 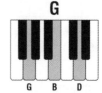

Words and Music by Danny O'Donoghue,
Mark Sheehan and James Barry

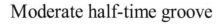

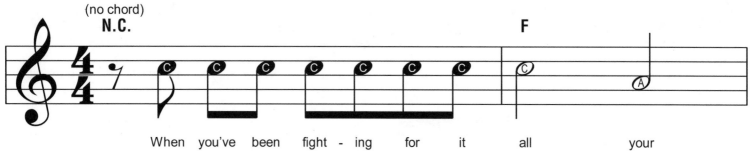

When you've been fight - ing for it all your

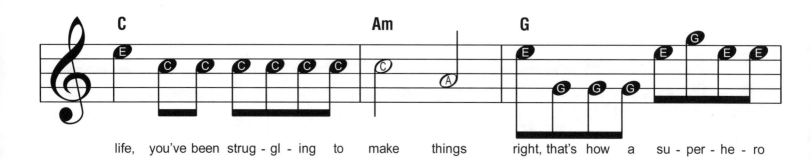

life, you've been strug - gl - ing to make things right, that's how a su - per - he - ro

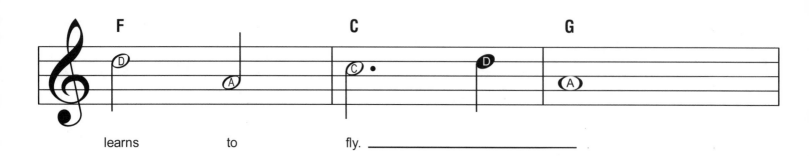

learns to fly. _____

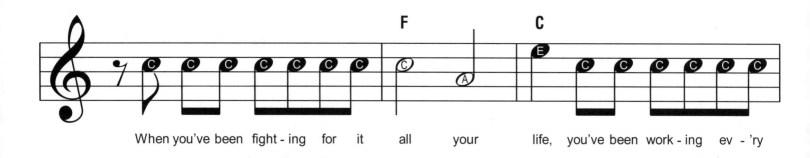

When you've been fight - ing for it all your life, you've been work - ing ev - 'ry

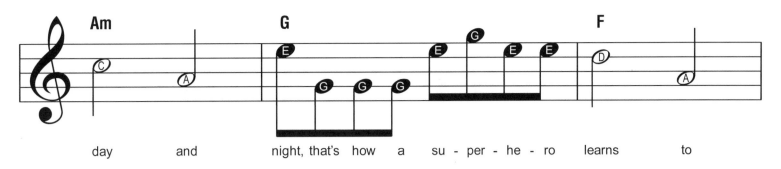

day and night, that's how a su - per - he - ro learns to

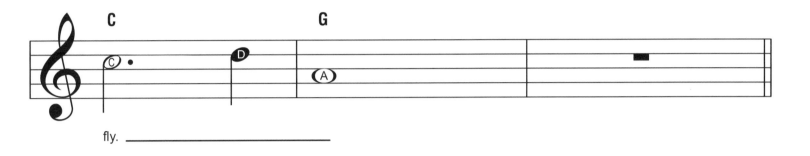

fly. _____

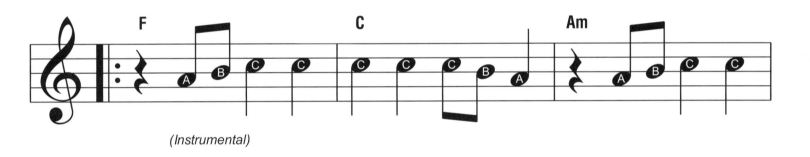

(Instrumental)

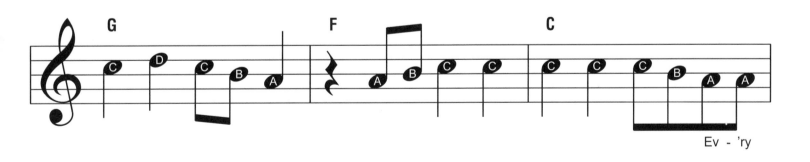

Ev - 'ry

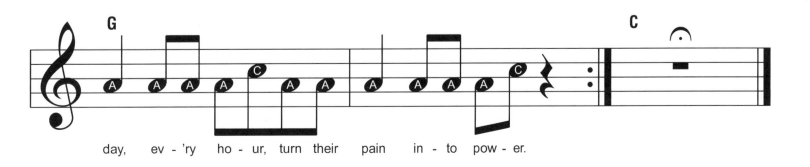

day, ev - 'ry ho - ur, turn their pain in - to pow - er.

There's Nothing Holdin' Me Back

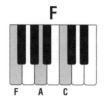 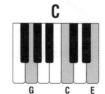 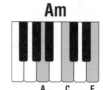 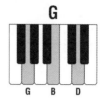

Words and Music by Shawn Mendes,
Geoffrey Warburton, Teddy Geiger
and Scott Harris

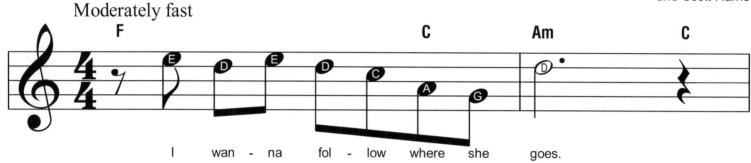

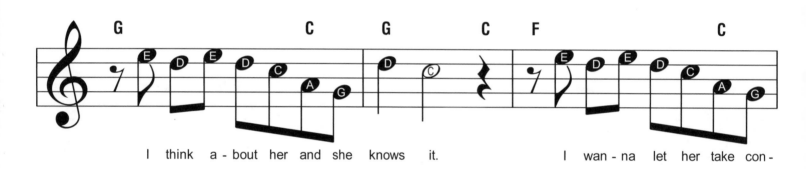

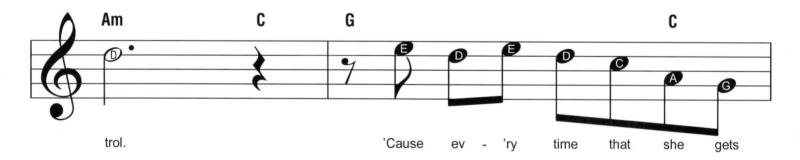

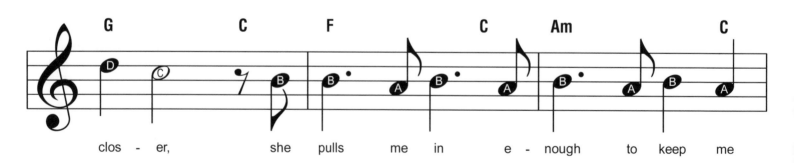

Treat People with Kindness

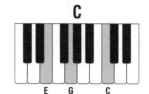 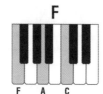 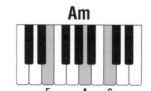 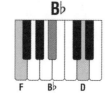

Words and Music by Harry Styles,
Jeffrey Bhasker and Ilsey Juber

May - be we can find a

place _____ to feel good, and we can treat peo - ple with

kind - ness. Find a place to feel good. I've got

a good feel - ing. I'm just tak - ing it all in.

Float - ing up and dream - ing, drop - ping

Wake Me Up

Words and Music by Aloe Blacc,
Tim Bergling and Michael Einziger

What About Us

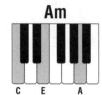
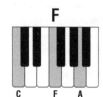
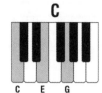

Words and Music by Alecia Moore,
Steve Mac and Johnny McDaid

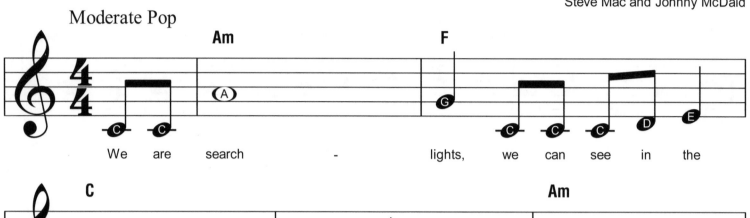

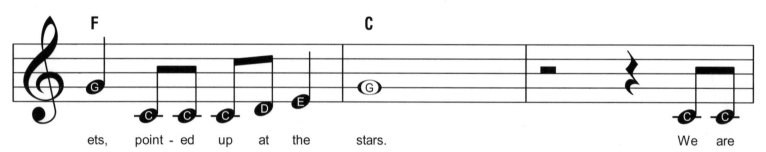

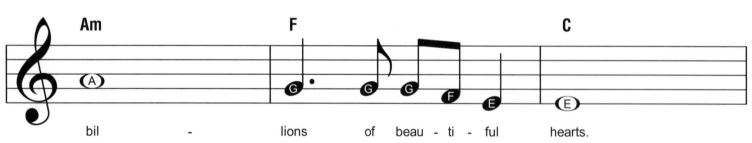

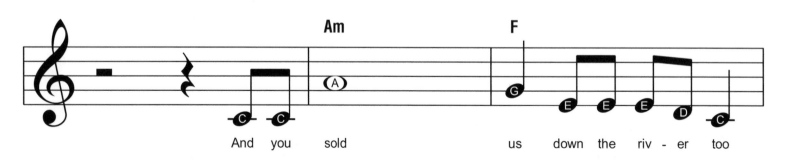

What Makes You Beautiful

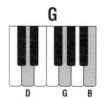 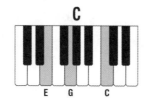 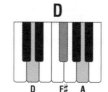 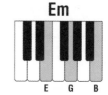

Words and Music by Savan Kotecha,
Rami Yacoub and Carl Falk

You're in - se - cure, don't know what for. You're turn - ing

heads when you walk through the door. _____ Don't need make - up to cov - er

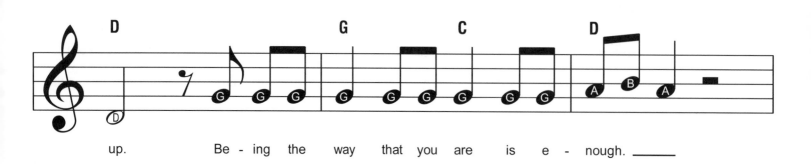

up. Be - ing the way that you are is e - nough. _____

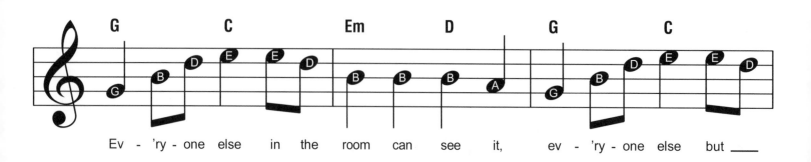

Ev - 'ry - one else in the room can see it, ev - 'ry - one else but _____

you. _____ Ba - by, you light up my world like no - bod - y else. The way that
If on - ly you saw what I can see, you'll un - der-

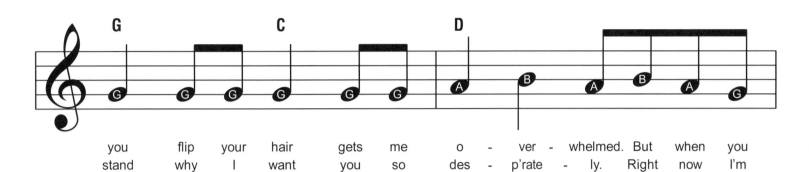

you flip your hair gets me o - ver - whelmed. But when you
stand why I want you so des - p'rate - ly. Right now I'm

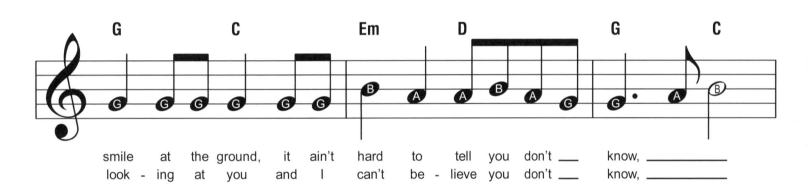

smile at the ground, it ain't hard to tell you don't ___ know, _____
look - ing at you and I can't be - lieve you don't ___ know, _____

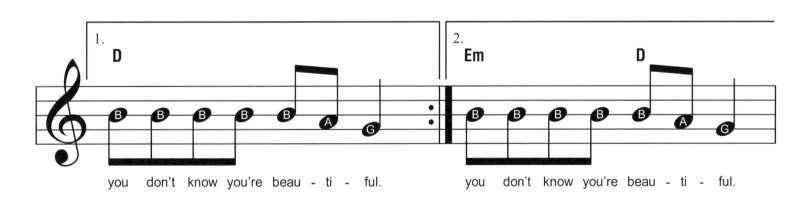

1.
you don't know you're beau - ti - ful.

2.
you don't know you're beau - ti - ful.

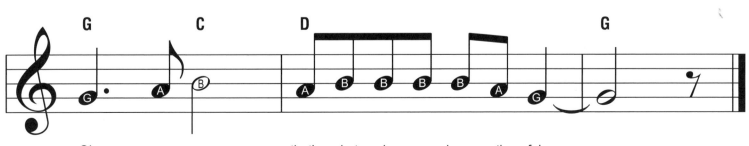

Oh, _____ that's what makes you beau - ti - ful. _____

You Can't Stop the Girl

from MALEFICENT: MISTRESS OF EVIL

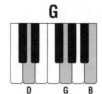
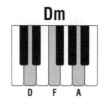

Words and Music by Bleta Rexha,
Nate Cyphert, Michael Pollack,
Alex Schwartz, Joe Khajadourian,
Sean Nelson, Jeff J. Lin,
Evan Sult and Aaron Huffman

Moderate half-time feel

Oh,   they're tryin' to shoot down an - gels.

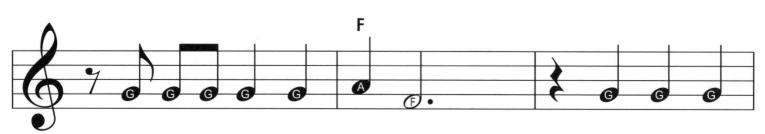

They're tryin' to pull their wings off   so they can't

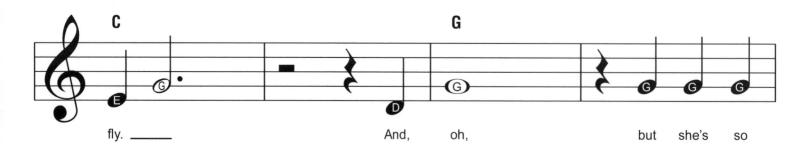

fly. _____   And, oh,   but she's so

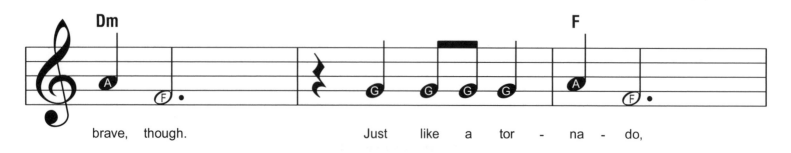

brave, though.   Just like a tor - na - do,

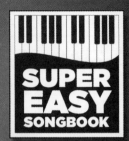

SUPER EASY SONGBOOK

It's super easy! This series features accessible arrangements for piano, with simple right-hand melody, letter names inside each note, and basic left-hand chord diagrams. Perfect for players of all ages!

THE BEATLES
00198161......................................$14.99

BEETHOVEN
00345533......................................$9.99

BEST SONGS EVER
00329877......................................$14.99

BROADWAY
00193871......................................$14.99

JOHNNY CASH
00287524......................................$9.99

CHRISTMAS CAROLS
00277955......................................$14.99

CHRISTMAS SONGS
00236850......................................$14.99

CLASSIC ROCK
00287526......................................$14.99

CLASSICAL
00194693......................................$14.99

COUNTRY
00285257......................................$14.99

DISNEY
00199558......................................$14.99

BILLIE EILISH
00346515......................................$10.99

FOUR CHORD SONGS
00249533......................................$14.99

FROZEN COLLECTION
00334069......................................$10.99

GEORGE GERSHWIN
00345536......................................$9.99

GOSPEL
00285256......................................$14.99

HIT SONGS
00194367......................................$14.99

HYMNS
00194659......................................$14.99

JAZZ STANDARDS
00233687......................................$14.99

BILLY JOEL
00329996......................................$9.99

ELTON JOHN
00298762......................................$9.99

KIDS' SONGS
00198009......................................$14.99

LEAN ON ME
00350593......................................$9.99

THE LION KING
00303511......................................$9.99

ANDREW LLOYD WEBBER
00249580......................................$14.99

MOVIE SONGS
00233670......................................$14.99

POP SONGS FOR KIDS
00346809......................................$14.99

POP STANDARDS
00233770......................................$14.99

QUEEN
00294889......................................$9.99

ED SHEERAN
00287525......................................$9.99

SIMPLE SONGS
00329906......................................$14.99

STAR WARS
00345560......................................$9.99

TAYLOR SWIFT
00323195......................................$9.99

THREE CHORD SONGS
00249664......................................$14.99

TOP HITS
00300405......................................$9.99

HAL•LEONARD®
www.halleonard.com